SHAMANISM

*YOUR PERSONAL JOURNEY TO
HEALING AND SELF-DISCOVERY*

About the Author

Mark Nelson is a resident shamanic practitioner at Shakti Healing Circle, one of the leading healing centers in Asia. He is a graduate of the Foundation for Shamanic Studies three-year program and a member of the Society for Shamanic Practitioners. He teaches workshops, provides shamanic services to clients, and leads apprenticeship programs.

SHAMANISM

*YOUR PERSONAL JOURNEY TO
HEALING AND SELF-DISCOVERY*

MARK NELSON

Llewellyn Publications • Woodbury, Minnesota

FIRST EDITION
First Printing, 2022

Book design by Valerie A. King
Cover design by Kevin R. Brown

Llewellyn Publications is a registered trademark of Llewellyn Worldwide Ltd.

Library of Congress Cataloging-in-Publication Data (Pending)
ISBN: 978-0-7387-6917-2

Llewellyn Worldwide Ltd. does not participate in, endorse, or have any authority or responsibility concerning private business transactions between our authors and the public.

All mail addressed to the author is forwarded but the publisher cannot, unless specifically instructed by the author, give out an address or phone number.

Any internet references contained in this work are current at publication time, but the publisher cannot guarantee that a specific location will continue to be maintained. Please refer to the publisher's website for links to authors' websites and other sources.

Llewellyn Publications
A Division of Llewellyn Worldwide Ltd.
2143 Wooddale Drive
Woodbury, MN 55125-2989
www.llewellyn.com

Printed in the United States of America

Disclaimer

CONTENTS

INTRODUCTION

This book provides an overview of shamanic theory and practice and is intended for those new to the subject, as well as being a reference for experienced practitioners. The text covers basics, including shamanic journeys, divination, shamanic healing, nature and nature spirits, and some intermediate topics such as shamanic dream work. Shamanism involves developing a working relationship with spirits and is highly experiential.

In each section, you are given an overview of a topic together with examples of key rituals, how you can do these, other rituals you can try yourself, and some pro tips. Example journeys are from attendees of shamanic workshops and are mainly presented without commentary, allowing the narrative to illustrate key points while preserving the richness of experiences (and the humor that is often involved in working with spirits).

If you feel you are not ready to perform any of the rituals described, come back to them later when you have more experience doing shamanic rituals. You can also seek training offered by recognized organizations and teachers. Details of these are provided at the end of the book.

An attempt has been made to use only cross-cultural rituals that do not involve cultural appropriation, but some culture-specific rituals are described where a ritual has been widely adopted outside of its original culture.

The term *shaman* describes a person working in a shamanic tradition and the term *shamanic practitioner* describes someone who is not part of such a tradition. Gender-neutral terminology is used as nouns such as *shaman* are generally applicable to any gender. A range of sexual orientations and practices such as cross-dressing are often seen in shamanic societies.

The terms *physical reality* and *spiritual reality* are used to differentiate the physical world that we live in and the spirit world. The term *client* is used to describe a person receiving shamanic healing, rather than *patient*, to distinguish shamanic healing from allopathic medicine. Shamanic healing is not a substitute for medical treatment; you should consult a medical professional if you believe that you have a medical or psychological condition.

The author is a graduate of the Foundation for Shamanic Studies three-year program of Advanced Initiations in Shamanism and Shamanic Healing and works as a shamanic practitioner at Shakti Healing Circle, one of the leading alternative healing centers in Asia.

CHAPTER 1
BASICS

Shamanism is a term that describes beliefs and practices of Siberian tribal peoples, but is now used more generally. Shamans and shamanic practitioners work with spirits, acting as an intermediary between spirits and a community, performing rituals like divination and healing. A key measure of their effectiveness is the recognition by their community of their results.

There are two main ways of working: a practitioner entering an altered state of consciousness to take a *shamanic journey* to spiritual reality to work with spirit—facilitated by drumming or other techniques—or allowing themselves to be voluntarily possessed by a helping spirit. You will learn how to safely do both types of work from this book.

Shamanism is not a religion, as it lacks a central authority, a book of teachings, and official places of worship. Some aspects of the role of a shaman are like that of a priest or priestess, but members of their community are encouraged to form their own relationship with spirit rather than the shaman interceding with spirit. There is no certification, but practitioners may serve in an apprenticeship. Teaching and initiation are mainly done by spirits.

The shamanic worldview is full of magic and wonder and is animistic. Everything is believed to have a spirit, including plants, tools, and natural phenomena. Everything is connected in a web that you affect and are affected by, with no separation between you, others, nature, and spirits. The main goals of rituals are the restoration of wholeness, balance, and harmony.

In the shamanic cosmology, spiritual reality is divided into the *upper world*, *middle world*, and *lower world*, which are connected by a vertical structure called the *world tree* or *axis mundi*. This structure may be used to travel between the worlds. The shamanic worlds all have a spiritual reality component; the middle world also has the physical reality component that we live in.

The lower world is not Hell (Hel is the Norse goddess of death), but instead is where we can meet ancestral spirits and power animals. The upper world is more ethereal and is where we meet human-like teaching spirits. The spiritual reality aspect of the middle world contains spirits like ghosts, who have not crossed over at death to where they should go. Some types of shamanic healing ritual are performed in the middle world, such as remote healing.

A BRIEF HISTORY OF SHAMANISM

Shamanism is ancient, dating back at least 70,000 years, apparent from rock carvings showing shamanic symbols and rituals recognizable to modern practitioners. It is a universal phenomenon with common rituals developing independently in different cultures, even where these were geographically separated. Such similarities are often explained as being due to common teachings by spirits rather than as a result of human migration.

In tribal societies, shamans helped people survive by interceding with spirits to get information, such as where game animals could be found. As agriculture developed, new rituals were used to ask or give thanks for abundant harvests. All tribal societies use plants medicinally.

Shamanism underlies and influences all spiritual and religious traditions. In parallel with the spread of organized religion, magical and folk medicine traditions developed. With human migration, these traditions spread around the world.

Shamanic practices were suppressed in many cultures and the scientific worldview sees shamanism as primitive superstition, but a shaman recognizes the limitations of the scientific worldview and its inability to explain the nature of reality. Shamanism, once universal, survived among indigenous peoples, especially in South America, Africa, Asia, and polar regions. A twentieth century decline in the popularity of Western organized religion led to a resurgence of pagan and other traditions, including shamanism.

What is the relationship between shamanism, witchcraft, and paganism? Witchcraft is a term used for practices that include rituals such as spells, inspired by ceremonial and folk magic. Paganism is a term for movements influenced by or derived from historical traditions such as Druidry. All these share some similarities with and are influenced by shamanism. Chaos magic, developed in the 1970s, strips symbolism and terminology from magical practices to leave a set of techniques that essentially derive from shamanic traditions.

There is growing interest in shamanism and the widespread availability of books, workshops, and courses. Western shamanic practice is influenced by cross-cultural or culture-specific rituals, leading to the use of terms such as *core shamanism* or *neoshamanism*. There is some criticism of cultural appropriation or exploitation, use of rituals outside their cultural context, and practitioners using rituals without training or initiation or claiming a heritage they do not have.

Shamanism can be applied to contemporary issues. New technologies provide opportunities to extend shamanic practices in ways our ancestors could not have imagined.

Types of Spirits

Some spirits are compassionate, some are amoral; others are ambivalent about, or hostile to, humans. The upper and lower worlds mostly contain compassionate spirits; the middle world also contains noncompassionate spirits and ghosts. Most cultures have one or more creator spirits or deities and spirits such as angels and demons.

A practitioner typically has several helping spirits that they work with, who can offer teaching, healing, and protection, either in a general sense or for specific types of work. A *power animal* is a helping spirit that provides you with power. Some spirits may be tricksters who mislead us, but who are important teachers and allies.

Human spirits include ghosts (with whom you should not be in a relationship with), *ancestral helping spirits* (who help descendants), and *ethnocentric spirits* (who are human spirits that return to protect and help a group such as a tribe or culture and may be hostile to those who act against their people or who do not respect sacred objects or places).

There are many spirits of nature, including spirits of animals, plants, minerals, mountains, rivers, and weather phenomena. Fairies are often viewed as nature spirits. Elemental beings are spirits connected to elements such as earth, air, fire, and water. Other spirits are spirits of directions or place, and spirits associated with astronomical objects like the moon and sun.

Called by the Spirits

People are called by spirit to be a shaman, not self-appointed. This involves going through *shamanic sickness*, which a person has to cure themselves of with the help of spirit. If the person is successful, there is then training and initiation by spirit. The person called to be a shaman is reborn a new person, able to serve their community. The sickness is a typical spiritual crisis. A person may refuse a call, or fail to cure the sickness, which typically leads to some form of misfortune in their life. They may, at a later stage, accept the call and succeed in curing the sickness. If they do not, they do not become initiated.

Of course, not all sickness is shamanic sickness and not everyone is called to be a shaman. Some practitioners work shamanically but may not have a true calling and may not have been initiated. Failure to have successfully gone through their own sickness and initiation means that a person may not be able to assist somebody going through an initiatory crisis.

You may feel that you are not called by spirit, you cannot do work for others, or you are not doing rituals correctly if you do not get results that match the examples described. You can still use journeying as part of your spiritual development, and spirit may initiate you! Try the practices described and keep doing the work as you are guided. You will be fine.

So, what does shamanic sickness look like for those who feel they may be experiencing it and how do they get through it? There are symptoms of illness, which do not progress as normal, respond to treatment, or go away of their own accord. Symptoms typically include:

1. Mental illness often confused with schizophrenia or hysteria. A person experiences altered states of consciousness which seem real. They may hallucinate, have visions, or hear voices. The person may lose contact with reality.

2. Behavior that rejects accepted norms and may be perverse or out of character. This can include addictions, wanting to be naked, and singing or dancing uncontrollably. A person may reject their ordinary life and seek solitude, often in nature or wilderness.

3. Physical illness such as chronic weakness, lethargy, seizures similar to epileptic fits, or eating disorders. Physical differences, such as having six fingers, are also associated with a shamanic calling.

4. Miscellaneous symptoms such as a person suffering misfortune. People feel they have something to offer or are part of something bigger than them. They may have out of body experiences, near-death experiences (NDEs), or even close calls with death.

Some symptoms may relate to physical reality illness, but a person undergoing shamanic sickness will feel the call deeply and know what they are experiencing is not normal illness. It is the contact by spirit that has chosen the person to be a shaman that causes the sickness. In a shamanic culture, this would be recognized by elders who would help the person by teaching them how to contact a helping spirit and enter and exit spiritual reality. The person can then journey to a helping spirit who will guide them. Today, the sickness often occurs outside a culture that recognizes the calling and validates initiation of a person as a shaman.

A person heals themselves by accepting the call and beginning a relationship with an initiatory spirit, which may cure the sickness, or learns from spirit how to heal it. An initiated human teacher may help. Initiation is done after relevant training by spirit in journey or vision.

Common motifs that are seen in a "typical" shamanic initiation include descent to the lower world to meet ancestors, ascent to the upper world to meet teachers, facing fears (especially of death), and suffering or tests. A person may undergo symbolic death in the journey, such as being dismembered, boiled, or burned. This does not involve pain. They are remembered (put back together), sometimes with extra parts or objects added. They are reborn as a new person.

The new shaman may gain power during initiation, as well as insights into the nature of reality. This may involve ecstatic experiences. They may meet spirits of diseases and learn how to diagnose and heal ailments. They are transformed, have wisdom, and can heal, guide the dead, and work to help a community. Teaching will continue by both spirit and human teachers.

The community that the new shaman is operating in would traditionally hold a ceremony that acknowledges their initiation and the acceptance of the new shaman by the community. In the present, such acceptance may take place over a longer time as the shaman develops a community, which in our connected world may consist of more than just a local community.

Pro Tips

The following tips are provided:

1. **Intention.** Effective ritual work is driven by a practitioner setting a strong intention. This is the most important factor in any work, including the rituals presented later.

2. **Working with spirits.** Show respect and express gratitude to spirits you work with. Working with spirit can be illogical; a practitioner works from the heart, not the head.

3. **Space and time.** Shamanic work is in sacred space and nonlinear time, where past, present, and future coexist, and we can influence remote or past and future events.

4. **Ethics.** You should obtain explicit, informed consent to work with others. Working without consent is sorcery and may result in karmic consequences or loss of power.

5. **Service.** Although a practitioner initially works on their own development, their focus should shift over time to working for the benefit of others in addition.

CEREMONY AND RITUAL

Ceremony and ritual are central to all spiritual work. You are familiar with ceremonies such as baptisms, weddings, and funerals, but may not know the difference between ceremony and ritual, and how to do them effectively. Rituals presented here, and any others you do, should be performed in a ceremonial context, which is why we deal with this topic first.

The terms *ceremony* and *ritual* are often used interchangeably but are different. A ceremony is an event that might mark a natural cycle or transition. Rituals include activities such as divination or healing. A ceremony is a container within which one or more rituals are done. A shamanic workshop is a ceremony; a shamanic journey at that workshop is a ritual.

A simple ceremony does not need a lot of preparation. It can just be creating sacred space, calling spirits, performing a ritual, and releasing spirits and sacred space. The structure of ceremonies is described on the following pages, and an example is provided for you to perform.

Clearing

Clearing is a ritual that removes unwanted energy from a space, person, or object. It typically involves burning plant material, such as herbs or incense, to produce smoke that fills a space, is directed over a person or object, or through which an object is passed. Clearing is done at the start and end of a ceremony. Herbs such as sage, or incense such as frankincense, are used.

Note that other herbs can be used for other purposes. For example, cedar may be used for purification and to attract positive energy, or mugwort may be used to promote trances, dreams, and visions. Clearing should be done with respect and gratitude to the plant spirits involved.

Herbs such as white sage and red cedar are sacred to First Nations, and if you use these, you should purchase from First Nations or Indigenous groups. White sage and palo santo are considered endangered but are not on the endangered species registry. A good all-purpose alternative is frankincense, which can be burned in incense stick or resin form. Try to use local plants you pick and prepare yourself (taking care to know which species are toxic), which helps you build relationships with local plant spirits.

For herbs, light the plant material and place it in a container (some traditions advise not using shells as containers). Allow herbs to flame and put out the fire by sweeping your hand or a feather fan over it. Sometimes herbs are bound together in a bundle or braided into ropes. Incense sticks can be burnt in an incense stick holder. For incense resin, use a fireproof container filled with sand or soil to dissipate heat. Light a charcoal disk, put it in the container, wait for it to turn gray, and carefully place resin on it (you may want to use metal tongs). Note that burning incense resin on a charcoal disk often produces a large quantity of smoke.

Clear the space you are working in, yourself, and ritual tools before and after use. Use plants associated with clearing and purification, set a relevant intention, and clear yourself by fanning smoke with a tool or your hand over yourself as you are guided. Be careful that embers do not fall onto skin, hair, or clothes. When you have finished, thank the plant spirits and place the materials in a fireproof container until extinguished. Ashes can be returned to the earth.

The Structure of Ceremonies

A general pattern is used for ceremonies with common activities. Note the symmetry involved. During a ceremony, energy is typically built to a peak and then released. Typical activities are:

1. Pre-ceremony activities

2. Creating sacred space

3. Opening the ceremony

4. Calling spirits

5. Performing rituals

6. Releasing spirits

7. Closing the ceremony

8. Releasing sacred space

9. Post-ceremony activities

Pre-Ceremony Activities

Pre-ceremony activities include deciding the ceremony's intention, rituals to include, and the timing and location. You can involve spirit in ceremony or ritual design, which lets you design your own ceremonies for specific intentions. You may clean a space or tools to be used in the ceremony, prepare an altar or fire and offerings to be made to spirit, and buy items such as candles, herbs, incense, and flowers. If used, an altar is usually placed in a cardinal direction and a fire in the center. For some ceremonies, you may abstain from certain food, alcohol, drugs, or sexual activity beforehand. You may perform some form of ritual purification of yourself and of any ritual clothing.

Creating Sacred Space

Create sacred space by clearing the space you are working in and clearing yourself. Visualize a circle around the space in a color of your choice and extend this into a three-dimensional sphere. You can draw a circle on the ground or place stones to delimit the sacred space, if you prefer. Set an intention that this circle demarcates sacred space and will keep unwanted energies out. Establish a focus for your ritual work at the center of the space, such as a fire, altar, or single candle. Always take appropriate precautions when working with fire.

Opening the Ceremony

A ceremony is opened with a short statement of intention(s). It can involve a speech, a song, a poem, any other kind of text, or an explanation of the ceremony's background and rituals. Opening the ceremony signals you intend to move from the physical and profane to the spiritual.

Calling Spirits

Spirits who take part in or help rituals are called in by a ceremony leader(s) and participants. This is done by asking them to join you with a statement such as, "I call my helping spirits into my ceremony to bless my rituals and assist me in my work." When you call spirits, there are often tangible effects such as temperature changes, sounds, or physical sensations.

Performing Rituals

Rituals are then performed. Note that clearing sacred space, opening the ceremony, and calling spirits are all examples of rituals. A ritual you should include is to make offerings to spirits with items such as foods, alcohol, flowers, or loose tobacco. Offerings can be placed on a small offering dish or bowl. As noted above, you aim to build energy to a climax and then release it in the rituals.

Releasing Spirits

When rituals are complete, thank the spirits you called into the ceremony and release them. Although you call spirits into a ceremony individually, you can release them collectively with a statement such as, "I thank the spirits for their assistance in my work and release you."

Closing the Ceremony

Close the ceremony by declaring or intending that it is complete. Extinguish a candle if one was used by snuffing out the flame (some traditions consider it disrespectful to blow a candle out). Closing the ceremony signals the intent to return to the physical and profane.

Releasing Sacred Space

Release sacred space by visualizing the removal of its container in an opposite way to how it was created. Remove objects used to physically demarcate sacred space unless these are to be reused at future ceremonies.

Post-Ceremony Activities

Post-ceremony activities can include dismantling structures used such as altars (if these are not to be reused), grounding activities such as eating and drinking, and activities that reinforce the ritual intention(s) such as a daily practice for a set period.

Example Ceremony and Ritual

The following is a simple ceremony you can perform to familiarize yourself with the approach, and for all the rituals in the book. The intention is to introduce yourself to your helping spirits and invite them to participate in your future work. This ceremony should take fifteen to twenty minutes.

1. **Preparation.** Prepare a space indoors or outdoors six to eight feet in diameter. This should be private and somewhere you will not be disturbed. You will need incense, an incense holder, a white candle, a candle holder, and an offering such as a flower. Have a notebook to record results. Prepare yourself by centering, grounding, and focusing on the intention.

2. **Create sacred space.** Light incense and clear the space with the intention that unwanted energies are removed from it and any wanted energies attracted to it. Visualize a circle around the space in a color of your choice and extend this into a sphere above and below you. Place a white candle in the center and light it. You should feel a change in the energy.

3. **Open the ceremony.** State that the ceremony is open. Say your intention: "I will introduce myself to my helping spirits and invite them to participate in my future ritual work."

4. **Call in spirits.** Call in your helping spirits by saying: "I call my helping spirits, teaching spirits, power animals, and ancestral helping spirits to join me and bless my rituals with their presence. I thank the spirits of place for allowing me to undertake this work."

5. **Ritual.** Say: "I express respect to my spirit helpers and ask that you guide, help, and protect me. I invite you into my life and give gratitude that you are willing to help in my spiritual development." Make an offering. You may receive a message. Dedicate the benefit of residual ceremony energy to your ancestors (or send it to the earth).

6. **Release spirits.** Release spirits by saying: "I thank my helping spirits for participating in this ceremony and release you to return to where you have come from."

7. **Close the ceremony.** State that the ceremony is compete. Extinguish the candle. Allow any incense that is still smoldering to burn out completely.

8. **Release sacred space.** Clear the space and release it by intending that the energy in the space is returned to its original state and by performing, in reverse, any visualization(s) or any other activities that you performed to create the sacred space.

9. **Post-ceremony.** Clear, center, and ground yourself. Make notes of what happened and any experiences or thoughts you had, messages or symbols perceived, and feelings you had. Pay attention to symbols that recur in ceremonies, which may be significant.

Pro Tips

The following tips are provided:

1. **Divination.** You can confirm via divination that rituals should be performed. Until you know how to do this, ask mentally if you should proceed and do as you are guided.

2. **Location.** Space should be private. Avoid public areas where you may affect or be affected by others. Do not work on private land without permission of a landowner.

3. **Timing.** Increase or attract energy when the moon is waxing; decrease or get rid of energy when it is waning. A new moon is a good time for new projects.

4. **Myth enactment.** Many rituals are based on myths and symbolically repeat a myth. Initiation rituals typically include symbolic death and rebirth.

5. **Symbolic acts.** Our subconscious cannot differentiate between actual and symbolic acts, so the latter can be used in ritual and may result in major transformations.

THE SHAMANIC JOURNEY

The shamanic journey often involves the use of aids, such as drums, to enter an altered state of consciousness and journey to spiritual reality, where you meet helping spirits and perform or participate in rituals to get wisdom, divination, healing, or initiation. In spiritual reality, the normal laws of space and time do not apply, and you can travel rapidly to any location and work with the past, present, and future. After completing work in spiritual reality, you return to physical reality with gifts for yourself or others. This section explains the journey process and what you can expect.

What is the difference between a shamanic journey, guided meditation, creative visualization, and dreaming? One difference is that a journey doesn't have preconceptions about what will happen, just an intention. This is different from guided meditation or creative visualization where there is a script and the focus is on a facilitator's voice. With journeying, you can go deeper into an altered state, are more in control of events, and remember the experience, unlike dreams. Symbols seen in journeys and dreams usually have the same meaning though.

Another question often asked is "How do I know I am not making up a journey?" There are two standard answers to this. First, go with the flow for now; you may find that journeys become progressively more real to you. Second, a sign that you are not making things up is when you get answers you do not like!

Some worry if journeying is safe, or if they can get stuck in a journey. It is safe; the worst thing that could happen is that you fall asleep during a journey. If journey content is upsetting, you can always ask a spirit to help you or return to physical reality by just intending to do so. Follow the instructions provided and you will be fine.

Most people are capable of journeying, some more easily than others. If you find it difficult at first, or do not experience similar results as those described in the examples, persevere and it should become easier. Note that it is possible to journey without using psychoactive substances; techniques like drumming can be used effectively to drive journeys.

So, why is drumming widely used to facilitate journeys and why is it effective? The sustained, repetitive rhythms used in drumming (or rattling, singing, or chanting) help create an altered state of consciousness by temporarily producing the theta brainwave state associated with deep meditation and trance. This is like the point between sleeping and waking where vivid (hypnagogic) images appear in your mind. It is in this theta state that shamanic journeys occur.

A journey is a ritual, so we perform journeys in a ceremonial context. Prepare by centering and grounding, establishing and clearing sacred space, and calling in helping spirits, as described on pages 11 and 12. When you complete your work, thank the spirits for their help, release them, and close the sacred space. Repeat the clearing to remove any residual energy from your ritual work.

The overall journey process consists of the following steps:

1. Prepare to journey

2. Set an intention

3. Phrase a question (if relevant)

4. Journey to spiritual reality

5. Perform rituals or other actions

6. Return to physical reality

7. Interpret the journey

Prepare to Journey

Use a room where you will not be disturbed. When you are learning to journey, lie in the dark or wear a blindfold, as it allows you to perceive spiritual reality more easily. You may eventually be able to journey while sitting, standing, or dancing. Wear comfortable clothes, have a device that allows you to play a drum recording, and use a pair of stereo headphones.

Set an Intention

Set an intention for the journey, which helps focus it. An intention can often involve asking a question, performing an action, or receiving healing. The stronger your intention, the more effective your work will be. It helps to state the intention in the present continuous tense (also called present progressive), which signifies that something is going to happen in the near future. For example, an intention could be "I am going to journey to the lower world to meet my power animal," or "I am going to journey to my helping spirit in the upper world to ask for a teaching."

Phrase a Question

Ask questions that are open-ended (cannot be answered with yes or no), precise, and use positive language. Start questions with *what, how, where* or *who* (avoid *when* or *why* questions). Ask one question per journey (unless you get a clear answer right away), otherwise you may not know what question an answer relates to. If you cannot think of a question, a good default one to use is "What do I need to know?" Another popular choice, especially for beginners, is "What is my life purpose?" You may though not get a clear answer to this question (or one that you like)!

Journey to Spiritual Reality

Listen to a drummer or a drum recording (shamanic drum apps are widely available). Specify the drumming length and *callback* duration (signal to return). Start with a journey time of ten to fifteen minutes and a callback of two minutes. Relax, close your eyes, listen to the drum, and focus on your intention. You should enter the journey state. You are often still aware of physical reality, but some people enter a deep trance where they are more aware of spiritual reality.

Journey to the lower, upper, or middle world using techniques described below. If you are distracted or nothing happens, refocus on the intention. If after five to ten minutes nothing still seems to happen, ask a question or intend an action anyway, or try to journey again later.

Most people experience spiritual reality visually, although some sense it in other ways. It may feel like a cartoon, and you may travel to different levels in, or move between, worlds. Spirit communication may be via telepathy, symbols, or sensations. Most people can ask questions and receive a response through words popping into their head.

Perform Rituals or Other Actions

Everything that happens in a journey is relevant and has significance or is part of the answer to a question. Often significant things happen at an early stage in a journey. If you end before the callback, do something else. In any work, ask yourself three questions: What else could I do? What am I not seeing? What other opportunities are there for healing?

Return to Physical Reality

When the journey ends, there is a change in the drumbeat, the callback. You will be aware of this (sensed even by those who fall asleep). You can choose to end a journey earlier if you have completed the intention. Finish what you are doing, thank any spirits you have worked with and return. You can retrace your steps or just come straight back. Open your eyes and take notes of the journey in a journal or use a recording device (which can also be used to narrate a journey). Review your journeys to identify recurring symbols or trends.

Interpret the Journey

Journeys are not interpreted literally. Ask yourself how symbols (nouns), events, or other responses relate to the intention. Over time, your personal symbology will become known to you and you can associate meanings with journey symbols. Then, consider the journey as a whole and try to infer the overall meaning. If you do not understand a journey's meaning, take another journey to a spirit and ask them to explain it in a way that you can understand. The output from one journey may help form the intention for the next journey. In this way, a series of journeys can be used as tasks that together lead toward an overall intention.

Note, we ask for guidance from spirit, not instructions. We do not just act on advice but ensure that decisions or actions feel intuitively correct and do not raise legal, moral or ethical issues. Compassionate spirits will never tell you to do something that may cause harm.

Key Rituals

People new to shamanism usually do two initial journeys: one to the lower world to meet a helping spirit (often an animal), the other to the upper world to meet a spirit teacher (often in human form). The methods used to journey to each world differ, so two key rituals are presented.

Journey to the Lower World

For the first example, the intention is to journey to the lower world to experience its nature, meet a helping spirit and ask a question (which you prepare before the journey). In the examples given, my student Carmen is using the question "What is my life purpose?"

> #### Carmen
>
> I went down a long way and then got in a boat. I traveled until I saw a waterfall. I went through this and there was a forest with an animal that was something like a lion. I asked that creature, "Are you my spirit?"
>
> It said, "No, I am not."
>
> Then I asked, "Where can I find my spirit?"
>
> It pointed somewhere else and asked me not to bother him. I kept walking and transferred into a boat again. It was dark. I traveled a long time and ended up sitting on the edge of a cliff. There was a very colorful bird beside me. I asked the bird, "Are you my spirit?" It did not reply to me but flew away and led me to another place, a white lighthouse on the top of a hill.
>
> I opened the door and saw a peacock. The peacock opened its tail. I asked the peacock, "Are you my spirit?" It did not reply to me, but I knew that it was my spirit. I asked it the question, "What is my life purpose?" It showed me a giant ship, similar to a pirate ship, but white in color. I got on that ship with the peacock and we went through a beautiful sea. We experienced a storm, but it became calm with beautiful sunshine. We landed on a white beach. I asked, "So, what does it mean?" It did not reply to me.

I guess the ship represents my life. I will go through good times and bad times, but at the end I will get to a better life if I can go through the storm in between. The beach is better than the previous place I am coming from, more positive, a better place.

Carmen experienced the lower world, met a spirit (peacock) that she intuitively knew was a helping spirit, but did not receive a clear answer to her question. She was shown a series of events that contain symbols she is meant to interpret. Key symbols include: the lighthouse, the white ship, the storm, and the white beach. Her interpretation is logical. There is not a right or wrong answer; the meaning, interpretation, and personal symbology are specific to her.

In your journeys, try to identify symbols and ask yourself what they mean. You should intuitively know. If you cannot interpret a journey, go back to spirit to ask them to do so. Be aware of opportunities presented in journeys. People are often led to a cliff edge or other high place. If you find yourself in such a location, one option is to jump off, to fly.

Journey to the Upper World

For the second example, the intention is to journey to the upper world to experience its nature, meet a spirit teacher, and ask a question.

Carmen

When I reached the upper world, I saw some traditional Chinese characters. I saw Kwan Yin. I asked her, "What is my life purpose?" She used the leaf she was holding to point to a cloud and the cloud disappeared. I didn't understand what she was trying to show me, and I asked her, "Can you explain more?"

Then a car drove me very quickly through a white beach to a place that looks like a palace. I went to the top of the palace and met a genie-like a cartoon character. It was a girl with big eyes. She was very cute. I asked her, "Are you my spirit guide?" and she smiled. I asked her, "What is my life purpose?"

She opened a window and showed me a part of a town where there were poor people, people who needed help. She told me, "Your purpose is to help those people."

I asked, "How can I help them? I do not have money to help myself."

A long, green Chinese-type dragon appeared. I rode on the dragon with the genie. The dragon took us to the place the genie showed me. The genie said, "Open up your hands." Things like gold and diamonds appeared. This meant the poor people have sufficient things and are okay. Then the dragon took us back to the palace.

The genie told me, "You have already got the power; you do not use it."

The dragon gave me a red crystal like a ruby. He said, "Keep this and the power will be with you." The genie went down to the sea and got a crystal also, a long one with a sharp point. It looked icy. She said, "You need to keep this for yourself."

Carmen met spirit teachers (Kwan Yin and the genie) and a power animal (dragon). She received clearer guidance and got specific information about her life purpose (to help the poor), even if she did not yet know exactly how she would manifest this. She had some ability that she was not currently using to help the poor. The gold and diamonds were symbols of how she will help them. She can find out more about this in other journeys. Do not worry if you do not receive such clear guidance. You will revisit this intention in later journeys.

The spirits also gave her *power objects*, which provide her with spiritual power (the ruby and crystal). If these are to be used in a specific way, this is explained to you when the objects are gifted. Often, objects simply empower you and you do not need to do anything with them. Do not worry if you do not receive power objects; you will later journey to obtain your own.

Other unusual things may occur in journeys. If you do not understand these, you can ask a spirit helper to explain them. You will also get more information as you see other examples later in the book, which may give you insights into earlier journeys you undertook.

How to Do the Key Rituals

Instructions for doing the two key rituals are given below. If you do not get results like the examples, do not worry. You can always undertake the journeys with the same intention again. Also, as you journey more, your ability to journey and results will improve in general.

Journey to the Lower World

To journey to the lower world, you travel into an opening that goes down through the earth (or water). A literary example of a lower world journey is *Alice in Wonderland*; Alice travels into a hole and arrives at a place where she meets talking animals. Imagine somewhere you know in nature as a starting point or start from the world tree. Methods used to go to the lower world include going into a hole or tunnel, climbing down the roots of a tree, traveling down a river or diving into water, going down a staircase, or being taken down by an animal.

Feel that you are moving though earth or water. If you are not successful, keep trying, perhaps changing how you descend. Do not be discouraged if you do not experience anything the first time. You usually see a tunnel of some sort, which leads to the lower world. The tunnel may bend and contain obstacles—you can get around or go through these by intending you can pass through them, changing size, changing into a small animal or using some other technique.

You eventually arrive somewhere. If you do not, ask your question anyway. For those who see their journeys, this may be a cave, garden, or natural landscape, in color or in black and white. Often something is waiting for you. If you see an animal or person, ask if it is your power animal or spirit guide. If they confirm they are, ask your question. If they are not, ask if they can show you where you can find an animal or guide (they may indicate a direction). If they are not helpful, or there is nobody waiting, move further into the lower world to look for a spirit. If you do not manage to find one, ask a question anyway or return and try again later.

Sometimes spirits test you. You may meet trickster spirits who intentionally mislead you (with good intention). Everything that happens is a teaching and learning experience. You will eventually succeed in contacting one of your power animals or other helping spirits.

When you ask your question, a spirit may answer telepathically, or it might show you something or perform some action. Try to remember the details of this. Significant things often occur early in a journey and may be missed.

You can go down to other levels in the lower world by looking for openings in the earth or other ways to travel down. You can also ask a spirit to show you how to go further down or to take you there.

If you get a clear answer to the question and the callback has not been given, you can return to physical reality or take the opportunity to explore the lower world or ask another question. When you hear the callback, return to physical reality the way you came or come back directly.

Typical experiences of going to the lower world:

> I went, down, down, down. It was like a lit-up tunnel…

> I go to the tunnel. It is bright and looks like a cartoon…

> I go down a spiral staircase…

> I got into this tree, it had a door, and then I went down. I was going down in a spiral. I started sliding inside this spiral…

> I got sucked into a tree and I dropped quickly in a downward spiral…

> I went into a cave and then down…

> I went down a well. I was swimming …

> I dived down a vertical reef cliff into an ocean…

Journey to the Upper World

To journey to the upper world, we travel upward. Classic motifs for upper world journeys are seen in *The Wizard of Oz*, where Dorothy goes up on a tornado, or *Jack and the Beanstalk*, where Jack climbs a magical plant. Begin at a high place in nature, such as a mountain or at the world tree. Methods used to go to the upper world include flying or being flown up by a bird or animal, rising on a smoke column, climbing a tree, traveling up a rainbow or on sun rays, entering the light on the horizon at sunset, climbing a staircase or ladder, climbing a rope or cord, jumping off of a mountain or some other high place, or going up on a tornado.

You know you have reached the upper world if you feel yourself passing through a porous membrane like a spider's web (if you do not go through this, you are still in the middle world). The upper world appears more ethereal than the lower world. People typically see images such as a white landscape, clouds, being on the top of something such as a mountain or pillar, a crystal city, a castle, etc. The light is usually brighter than in the lower world.

When you arrive, there may be a spirit waiting for you. If so, ask the spirit if it is your teacher. If they confirm that they are, then ask your question. If they are not, ask them if they can show you where your teacher is. If they are not helpful or if nobody is waiting when you arrive, then move further into the upper world to look for your spirit. If you do not manage to find it, ask a question anyway or return and try again later.

When you return, the question could be more divinatory or asking what you can do to heal a condition. You may even receive a healing from spirit. You can also repeat the question you asked in the lower world if you did not get an answer you understood or ask for more information about the previous answer.

Sometimes, spirit teachers seem distant or difficult to talk to. This may be a test to see how committed you are to working with them. By showing respect and persevering, you will make them receptive to you. Use courtesy when addressing teachers and respect their opinion if they make reasonable requests.

You can go to other levels in the upper world by looking for ways to ascend or ask a spirit to show you how to go further up or to take you. When you hear the callback, retrace your steps and return to physical reality. You can do this before the callback if your journey is complete.

Typical experiences of going to the upper world:

> I flew and passed the clouds. I flew on a big bird…

> I saw a white bird, a phoenix. I held on to it and flew to the sky through the cloud…

> I saw a flock of birds. I was climbing a tower and they came and swept me up…

I was a white eagle flying up…

I ran up a snowy steep mountain. I ran and ran and saw something I passed through…

I was climbing up the roots of a banyan tree…

Other Rituals

Other rituals that you can perform include: journey to the middle world, journey to meet your true self, journey to your sacred place, and journey to find out your life purpose

Journey to the Middle World

The intention is to journey to the middle world to explore its nature.

We perform some types of healing in the middle world and can also use a middle world journey to find lost people or objects. The middle world appears similar to physical reality but often looks surreal, vivid or confusing. In the lower and upper worlds, we usually meet only compassionate spirits, but in the middle world we can meet any type of spirit, including ghosts and malevolent spirits. A power animal can accompany you to act as a protector.

To journey to the middle world, leave your physical reality location horizontally and continue in the middle world rather than traveling vertically. We stay on or above the surface of the world. If you are in a room, you can visualize leaving through a door or window. In an initial middle world journey, you should briefly explore the middle world. You can converse with a spirit you meet there if you feel this is appropriate. At the end of the journey, return to physical reality by intending to come back to your body and focusing on returning to physical reality.

An example middle world journey:

Carmen

This time it was more fragmented; I went to different places. I went to a jungle and felt a lot of animals were around me hiding in the bushes. I flew over the treetops and saw a lot of birds flying with me. There was a rainbow creating a bridge for me to walk across. My dragon then appeared and brought me to a place that was cold and snowy.

I landed there and walked through the snow to a little cottage. An old woman opened the door and invited me to go inside. There was an old man and a fire beside them. They offered me a hot drink, which I drank. They were being kind to me. Then I left and they smiled and said goodbye.

My dragon then took me to a beach. There was a pier where I could walk out over the water. There were a lot of what looked like ghosts trying to pull me down; they wanted to pull me down, but I felt that with the power animal there they could not really approach me or touch me.

The middle world can be confusing and contain spirits who are not always compassionate. Here, Carmen's power animal performs two of its usual roles, transportation and protection.

Journey to Meet Your True Self

The intention is to meet our true self in order to find out about it and how to work with it. A destination world is not specified. Go to where you are guided and do this for all other journeys, unless a preferred destination is stated.

You can journey to your true self, and work with and build a relationship with it. Your true self wants to help you. Ask it for guidance to help you achieve your potential, on how to live as you should were it not for things like life events, your ego, and limiting beliefs diverting you or getting in your way. By adopting the nature of your true self, you achieve balance and harmony. Working with the true self may not be easy; you may need to let go of some beliefs!

Salina

I was high up in the mountains. It was misty, and I saw a guy that looked like a Greek god. He took me to my true self, who looked like me when I was five or six. He told me some things that I already knew, what I have to do, and he answered a question I had, saying that I was nostalgic for my childhood and needed to let go of that to be able to move forward. I asked about my purpose and it is always the same thing: creating.

Journey to Your Sacred Place

The intention is to journey to a place sacred to you and learn how it can benefit you.

Sue

It was a tree, a very ancient tree, like a big redwood. The roots were massive, spread out, and very anchored. I asked what the significance of the tree was and how I would use it, and was told it is a channel, a connection between upper and lower, a place to go to explore, rest, ask questions, talk with others, whatever you need. I went into the tree and was enjoying solitude. I said, "What should I do?"

It said, "Crack open the chrysalis and get out." I did not want to and argued, but eventually broke out and came out the hole I entered by. There was lots of light. I have been hidden away for a while, withdrawn, and know I want to be less insular. It mirrors what is happening in my life.

A tree often appears in this journey. This is a symbol of the world tree, which allows you to connect to different realms. In the example, Sue is encouraged to bring her light into the world.

Journey to Find Your Life Purpose

The intention is to journey to the find out what our purpose is in this life.

Lilian

There were three broad areas: to help and to heal by taking money from the rich and transforming it so it helps the poor and healing myself so I can heal others, to find joy and peace within myself no matter what is outside, and to ring the sound of a true bell. To be the first to stand up and say something that is true, and by doing so giving others permission to make the same sound.

Pro Tips

The following tips are provided:

1. **You are in control.** You are in control during a journey and can return at any time.

2. **Intensity.** Over time, journeys become more vivid, spiritual reality more tangible, and your work more effective. A richer journey experience is created by using multiple senses.

3. **The future.** A journey may tell you about a possible future. If you do not like this, decide on an alternative and journey to ask what changes you need to make to manifest that future. Destiny is not fixed. Manifest the best future for you.

4. **Journey frequency.** You should journey a few times a week. If you journey too often, you do not have time to apply guidance you have received in your life and see results.

5. **How do I know where to go?** When you start, you usually work with teachers who advise you. As you become more experienced, you set your own intentions. In general, if you plan to work with power animals or ancestors, go to the lower world. If you plan to work with teachers, go to the upper world. Some work occurs in the middle world.

SHAMANIC POWER

Power is gifted from spirit. Power can be lost, but can also be restored or acquired. Restoring, keeping, and growing power is key to your development and being able to help others. Shamanic power should be used wisely and responsibly. One of the best-known shamanic rituals is *power animal retrieval*, which you can do for yourself and others. After people have learned to journey, power animal retrieval is usually the next ritual that they experience.

You may read that someone else needs to retrieve your power animal for you, but it is possible to retrieve a power animal yourself, which is the key ritual presented here. You will learn both approaches. You or your helping spirits can perform most rituals on your behalf without the need for a practitioner to guide you, although a practitioner is useful for some types of ritual or when a person does not know what their issues are or how to proceed in resolving them.

Power Loss

Power can be lost several ways, unintentionally or intentionally. You may give power to others or power may be taken from you. You lose power if you are disconnected from nature or lose soul parts. Spirits may also abandon you if you breach taboos or practice sorcery. You should view bad experiences as lessons you can learn from and make changes to improve things, rather than being affected by them. You are in control of your destiny and can change your life if you want. You should be aware of the effect the views of others and stories have to empower or disempower you and make changes to stop being disempowered in this way.

Symptoms of power loss include feeling lethargic, unmotivated, powerless, or at the mercy of others. You may not be able to move on from relationships or move forward in your life. Power loss can lead to physical, emotional, or mental issues, or being unable to fulfill your life purpose. Benefits of retrieving or acquiring power include an increase in energy and feeling more in control of your life, as well as healing physical, emotional, mental, and spiritual issues. It also makes it harder for others to take your power, allows you to make positive changes in your life, and to be more authentic and aligned with your destiny.

Power Acquisition

So, how do you get power? Power is obtained from shamanic journeys, dreams, power animals, other spirits, elements, natural phenomena, vision quests, and initiations. A spirit can empower you or it can act as an intermediate between you and power. Power is acquired in rituals such as power animal retrieval and can be accumulated over time. Power can also be provided via power objects, songs, and dances. Spending time in nature is also empowering.

Power objects are given or shown to us in journeys and contain or connect us to power. Where an object is seen in a journey may coincide with where it may be acquired in physical reality. A physical object may not look the same as in a journey but is recognized by its energy. Power objects are used to raise power in rituals, and include objects like feathers, rocks or crystals. A power object may not be what you expect, but be open to, and grateful for, objects you receive.

Power songs and dances can be given by spirits. Songs, words, or tones carry power and can be used in healing rituals. Dances can be used to raise power in a ritual. You can also merge with spirit during dance. Power songs and dances are often simple and repetitive, having the same effects as drums.

Power Animals

Our ancestors lived closer to nature, were familiar with animal behavior, and worked with animal spirits. Several terms are used to describe animal spirits. A *power animal* is a helping spirit who provides power. A *totem animal* is a spirit that acts as a guardian and symbol of a group, family, or tribe. Some clans believe that they are descended from a clan totem animal.

Everybody has multiple power animals. An animal may be with you your whole life or come and go as needed, usually providing a trait that is useful to you. At any time, you may have several power animals. A power animal may leave if you do not work with or respect it, causing disempowerment and making you vulnerable to illness and misfortune. If someone is depressed, weak, or illness prone, it may be a symptom that they have lost a power animal.

Power animals are a source of power, guidance, protection, and companionship. They help you when you journey and can introduce you to other spirits. The power animal provides protection in both spiritual and physical reality, teaches you knowledge and wisdom, may give you enhanced abilities, and often acts as a means of transport in spiritual reality. Power animals may also perform rituals such as divination or healing for you or others.

A power animal has the appearance, character, and behavior of a physical or mythical animal, but is an archetypal spirit. A power animal is usually a wild or mythical animal, not a domestic one. The animal species may or may not be native where you live, or to your culture. You can work with any animal that wants to work with you and that has gifts for you.

A power animal has human qualities, such as being able to speak, and supernatural capabilities, such as the ability to shape-shift into other forms or behave in ways a physical animal cannot. For instance, a land animal may be able to fly or breathe underwater in spiritual reality. Power animals are often thought to reside in the lower world but can travel to any location.

Shamanic work depends on developing ongoing relationships with spirits. A power animal is one of a practitioner's primary spirit helpers and often accompanies them in journeys. Power animals may appear in journeys, dreams, meditations, or visions. Seeing repeated images of an animal is an indication it is appearing in your life to call your attention to it. When we begin to work with a power animal, we also notice it more frequently in physical reality media.

You should honor and respect a power animal and thank it for being in your life. Ask it why it wants to be a power animal for you, how you will work together, how you can represent it, what offerings it likes, and what you can do for it. Do not always just ask for help from a power animal. You should accept a power animal you receive. Sometimes people feel they should have a particular animal or do not like or want to work with the animal retrieved, especially if they do not view it as powerful, but all power animals have valuable gifts and teachings.

You may have a fear of phobia of an animal, such as snakes or spiders. Working with a power animal helps overcome fear of the physical animal. Transforming fear or discomfort into a relationship with the animal is powerful and healing. If you really cannot work with an animal, you can politely ask that you be allowed to work with another one and perhaps return to the animal in the future, but this would be a missed opportunity. Spirit will not present something to you that you cannot handle, no matter how uncomfortable or difficult it seems.

There are several ways of working with a power animal once it has been retrieved. You can ask it to meet you in journey, dream, or meditation. Get to know it by asking it to show you its traits and what it can teach you. Research the animal and see what others say about it and how to work with it, being guided by what feels right for you. Gifts that a power animal brings may be different for you than other people; power animals have multiple traits and abilities.

You can also research the physical animal. Learn about its behavior and traits it has. Other things to consider are donating to relevant charities or volunteering to help animals. You may involve a power animal in ritual practice. Objects representing power animals can be put on an altar or carried. These can be simple objects like a candle or picture or an object that you paint, draw, or sculpt. Animal parts are also used on altars, costumes, tools, and power objects.

Try to experience the world as your power animal does, using its senses. You will learn rituals where you shape-shift into or merge with a power animal. In shape-shifting, you change yourself into the animal form (in spirit). When you merge with a power animal, you are voluntarily possessed by a spirit that is in this form. The experiences are different, as will be explained on the next few pages.

It is often believed that power animals should not be revealed to others. It is, though, usually acceptable to reveal animals in a teaching context.

Shape-Shifting

Shape-shifting is the ability to change form into an animal or bird and back. This is a symbolic, not physical, transformation widely seen in mythology, folklore, fairy tales, and popular culture. Transformation can be a punishment from gods. Sometimes a being transforms to escape a pursuer. In folklore, we see shape-shifting in tales of werewolves and vampires. We can perform shape-shifting in spiritual reality for several purposes:

1. To obtain power and abilities associated with the form.

2. To experience a form and get to understand the animal.

3. To have a deep sense of communion with the form and with nature.

4. As a method of transport or to overcome obstacles in spiritual reality.

5. To assist us in changing ourselves, our worldview, and our external relationships.

To shape-shift we invite the energy and consciousness of a form into us. It helps to experience the world as that being does, using as many senses as possible. Masks, costumes, or skins are used as a focus to help shape-shift (putting on the costume, mask, or skin begins the process).

Responsible Use of Power

Power is usually received as a gift rather than being sought. It is used for yourself and others wisely and responsibly. Power can be intoxicating and can lead to its inappropriate use. Be careful of your relationship with it and its use, and especially avoid performing sorcery. You know intuitively if rituals you perform are for the good of yourself and others or if they are not. The proper application of spiritual power is not domination and exploitation of others or things; such abuse can result in power loss as spirits withdraw their assistance from you. Focus instead on how power can be used to develop, empower, and enable yourself and others.

Key Ritual: Journey to Retrieve a Power Animal for Yourself

The intention is to journey to retrieve a power animal yourself or to ask one of your helping spirits to do a power animal retrieval for you.

Maya

In my very first shamanic journey, I kept seeing ants. We were dancing in the lower world. Sometimes I see the same ant in my house, and it is not normal the way it behaves. The other night I was sitting there, and it was standing on its legs waving its antennae at me. I was like, "What do you want, man? You gotta talk to me, I don't know what you want." Obviously, it was trying to communicate with me.

I journeyed to retrieve it. It was so cool. I went to the lower world, and the ant was right there waving its antennae again. He said he has been trying to get my attention for years! "That was me. When you see me, you have to pay attention to images that come into your head at that time. It is better to do a meditation or whatever you need to do to be open to a vision and pay attention to the images, which are warnings for you or other people."

I asked how I would understand the meaning and he said it would be in the vision. There was some kind of fire in one of the visions, a lot of fire. I asked, "What did you mean by that vision?" He flashed up the image of the forest burning.

I thought I would need to gather him up, but he just crawled right into my skin and up my arm on the inside. He was big but when I said, "Let's work together," he just shrank and went into my skin.

Ants are amazing. They have strength, stamina, dedication, and community. After that journey, I thought, "Oh my God! That is what I want to do, community building."

How to Do the Key Ritual

Instructions for doing the key ritual are given on the next few pages. Again, if you do not get results similar to the example above, do not worry. You can always undertake the journey again. If you feel that you need help, you can arrange to see a practitioner who can retrieve a power animal for you.

For this type of ritual, set the intention for retrieving a power animal that wants to work with you. Retrieve only one animal in this journey. You are not usually journeying with an intention to retrieve a specific animal unless you feel strongly this is an animal you are to work with, and spirit confirms this during the journey. You usually journey to the lower world, but you may be guided to go to the upper world. Journey to the world you are guided to.

A power animal or other helping spirit should be waiting for you. If one is not waiting for you, then search until you find one. Confirm that a spirit is your power animal or a helping spirit. You will know intuitively if the answer is true. If you are in any doubt, then do not proceed but come back to physical reality and try again later.

If you meet a spirit who will perform the power animal retrieval, they may have the power animal with them or may ask you to wait and go to find it for you. They will then put the power animal in one of your chakras, usually the heart chakra. The spirit may place the animal in you, blow it into you, or invite the animal to run, fly, or dive into your energy body. They may then seal it in you. Return to physical reality, bringing the power animal with you.

The other method is to meet the power animal and invite it to merge with you in spiritual reality and then return with it. The animal may enter a chakra or simply merge with you. If it does not do this, you can reach out and pull the spirit into your body. Again, return to physical reality with the power animal as above.

Accept the animal unless you are guided strongly that you do not want to work with the animal for some reason, which should not be the case.

A general rule is not to have insects as power animals, but ants, bees, and butterflies can be power animals.

You might want to begin your work with the power animal by exploring its energy, perhaps by moving as it guides you to move. You will feel energized and may have slight trouble sleeping the first night or so as you get used to the spiritual power you are now holding.

Other Rituals

Other rituals that you can perform include:

1. Journey to retrieve a power animal for another person.

2. Journey to shape-shift into a power animal.

3. Journey to learn how to merge with a power animal.

4. Journey to learn a power animal song or dance.

5. Journey to your seat of power.

6. Journey to find and remove power blocks.

7. Journey to find a power object.

You can also journey to find out how you give your power away or take power from others.

Journey to Retrieve a Power Animal for Another Person

The intention is to journey to retrieve a power animal that wants to work with a person, or can be more specific, such as to find a power animal that wants to work with them to address a particular issue. You may lie beside the person during the journey. The person for whom the animal is being retrieved does not journey.

The practitioner looks for an animal and waits to see several perspectives or representations of it to confirm it is the person's animal. This usually involves seeing different sides of the animal. When a power animal has been found, clutch it to your chest in spiritual reality or place it in your heart chakra, or a tool like a crystal, and return with it to physical reality. The energy of the power animal is then blown into the person's heart and crown chakras. You can scoop energy out of your heart chakra with your hands and blow the energy into the person through your hands. Seal the power animal in by shaking a rattle over the two chakras as guided.

Tell the person what animal has been retrieved and explain to them how to work with it. You might want to advise the person to conduct their own research into the meaning a power animal has for them, rather than just read a description of this from a book.

Mark

> I journeyed to a lower world beach, which is ironic as the journey was being performed in the Australian outback! A whale was swimming rapidly from side to side. It was waiting and it was clearly impatient. The whale saw me, fixing me with its eye. It raced to the shore, rising out of the water until it was flying toward me through the air. I wondered how I was supposed to embody this leviathan. I reached out my arms and, as it approached me, it got smaller until I could place my hands around its body and guide it into my heart.

Here the whale is seen from two sides and from the front. You might see symbols or other representations of an animal, such as a photograph, painting, statue, film, or cartoon.

Journey to Shape-Shift into a Power Animal

The intention is to journey to a power animal in spiritual reality, find out how to shape-shift into it, and then shape-shift to explore its nature. Shape-shifting occurs in spiritual not physical reality. In journeys, you can transform into an animal to overcome obstacles, perhaps by changing size to get through small spaces.

Having shape-shifted into the animal, explore moving as the animal does through its habitat or taking part in behavior like stalking and hunting prey. Shape-shifting allows you to develop a deeper connection with a power animal and can be used in other journey contexts. Shape-shift back into your own form before returning from the journey.

Dawn

Dragon showed me how to shape-shift. My dragon is very naughty and turned into a chicken. I became a dragon.

He was trying to get me to feel and hear the air and the surroundings using senses that he has. Then we started flying. We were over a river and he blew out air that created waves. In another scene we went to a snowy place, I blew out fire, and it became a muddy, watery land that I could touch and feel.

Journey to Learn How to Merge with a Power Animal

The intention is to journey to a power animal in spiritual reality, find out how to merge with it, and then merge with it to experience its power. The other challenege is to unmerge with the animal—in a way it advises you to—and ask how to merge with it in physical reality.

Spirit merging empowers and facilitates healing and other work. Some healing modalities like *extraction healing* involve merging with a power animal in physical reality. We usually merge with one spirit at a time, often a specialist spirit. Each time you merge, you acquire power and increase your capacity to carry spiritual power. Merging is temporary. Long-term merging is not recommended as it interferes with normal activities. Merging can be done in two ways:

1. **Physical reality merging.** Call the spirit to join you and ask it to merge. Spirit presence is usually perceived by temperature change, goose bumps, or similar sensations.

2. **Spiritual reality merging.** Journey to a spirit and ask it to merge with you in journey. You can then work in spiritual reality or return to physical reality with a merged spirit.

You unmerge by having this intention and then stepping away from the merged spirit or shaking its energy off of you, or as you are guided or shown by a helping spirit.

This type of merging is not the same as being possessed and you remain in control. When you merge with an animal, you usually experience sensations like an energy increase, feeling the presence of the animal, and wanting to move like the animal or imitate its cry.

Ryan

The way I merge with horse is he rears up and puts his legs in my body. I use his sense of smell and sensitivity to find things. I unmerge with him as if I were taking off a cloak.

Journey to Learn a Power Animal Dance or Song

The intention is to journey to the animal to learn a song and/or dance that you can use in physical reality to deepen your relationship with it or for purposes such as healing.

Having merged with a power animal in physical reality, you can "dance" the animal. Do this unconsciously, moving how the animal wants to move. This can be done alone or in groups, in silence or with drumming or rattling. Dancing the animal forms a strong connection with it.

Siobhan

I got a physical sensation in my abdomen. There was a song involved with the womb. It was for fertility and healing negative energy stored around the womb, for example, as a result of miscarriages or stuck energy.

Journey to Your Seat of Power

The intention is to journey to your seat of power. This is a power source that can be visited as needed for empowerment. I often leave the intention a bit vague, so people are not given preconceptions about what their seat of power is.

Ann

I asked for the seat of power and there was nothing. I thought the seat of power was inside me, so why was I looking for it outside of me? All of a sudden, from underneath, my back jolted. It felt as though it was real. A Victorian chair with an uncomfortable back jolted me up. I was sitting in it and felt like I was in the room here.

I said, "This is uncomfortable."

"No problem, we'll stick a strap around you."

> So, I am strapped in really uncomfortably. I thought
> don't fight this. You had only just started drumming
> and I thought I will be like this for fifteen minutes!
> Then I started to grow like Alice in Wonderland
> and the chair was growing and I felt really good.

As you can see from Ann's journey, your seat of power often takes the form of some kind of seat. One interesting thing about this journey is people often go to an object like a chair and walk around it, clean it, or take some other action—anything other than sit in it! This shows a reluctance to stand (or sit) in their power. If this happens, I ask people to go back and sit in it (or perform an equivalent action). The point is to positively engage with your seat of power.

If people are avoiding their power, they need to consider why that is. Perhaps it is one or more limiting beliefs stopping them using their power. Having done this journey, people know where to find their power when they are ready to access it.

Journey to Find and Remove Power Blocks

The intention is to journey to find out how our power is blocked and to remove the block(s). You often feel disconnected from your power, or that there is some sort of block impeding it. Blockages are often represented via symbols like rope, vines, rocks or metal.

Sue

> There is some block that stops me being what I could be. I am scared of what I would become. I fear I have mis-used power. I got views of times when I was a medicine woman or witch. I have seen this in dreams. I seemed to be in mediaeval times as a medicine woman. I have often dreamed of her. She lived on her own in the forest.
>
> When people needed help, they would go to her, give her an offering and she would sort them out. She was a lonely woman, but a very gentle soul. I can see the block; it is a great big black granite block that sits near her. I asked my spirit, "What is the block, how can I clear it, what's going on and who created it?"

"You created the block in the past after this woman's life, because you were fed up with giving of yourself all the time, always helping others and missing out on things others take for granted."

I was trying to remove the block, walking around it and trying different things. It got smaller but there is an angry core to it. It shrank but did not go. I feel that it would change my life if it did. It will give me work to do. I do want to remove it. I have got to the point now where it needs to go, it's holding me back.

Sue undertakes a second journey to completely remove the block. She does this by intending to re-join the journey at the point that she left to continue it.

Sue

It was quite emotional. As soon as I went, there was a path of spirits leading to the forest where I was before. It was like a procession. Everybody was happy. I could feel the love coming from everything. I made my way up the passageway and came to the block which had pretty much disappeared by that point. It became like a seat and I was told to sit down in it.

You could see the black stone underneath, but it was alive with light, sparkling. Then I was raised above and was looking down and the spirits were beginning to surround it. I felt myself sitting very firmly in the seat. The seat then broke apart and became light and sparkles. Everything combined and joined together, the spirits, stone and me. And spread out.

It felt like there was a small pebble left and I stayed a bit longer and asked them to help me get rid of this. Then it came straight into my heart, everything was coming in, like golden star light. I asked for it to spread throughout my body and it felt like the other spirits were coming in as well to help integrate and build and explore my own power and where it will go. I feel good.

Journey to Find a Power Object

The intention is to journey and ask to be shown a power object in spiritual reality that we can receive as a spiritual power object or which will appear to us in physical reality. Ask to be shown how to use the power object and if there is anything else you need to know about it.

> #### James
>
> I went to a stream in Hokkaido. There is a rock in the stream I am to bring back and put on my desk. It has to do with the power of Bear, Hokkaido being the home of the Ainu people. This rock is to do with the energy of Hokkaido, the energy there is good for me. A Bear came, slashed my belly, put my skin on himself, and laughed.

Wearing your enemy's skin is a motif often seen in myths, legends and stories. Bear is parodying this, but there is also an initiatory element to this journey.

Pro Tips

The following tips are provided:

1. **Power animal form.** Do not overly anthropomorphize (humanize) a power animal. Be open to the animal expressing itself and communicating to you in its own way.

2. **Eating power animals.** Is it taboo to eat a species that is your power animal? In some cultures, it is and killing and eating the animal may result in its power being withdrawn; in others it is not. Meats such as horse and whale are taboo in some cultures but eaten in others. If you feel eating your power animal is wrong, then do not eat it.

3. **Wild animals.** A power animal is not dangerous to you; it is a source of power. It wants to work with you. When encountering an animal in the wild, remember that it is a wild animal and may well be dangerous, even if it is your power animal!

4. **Representation.** You can wear a costume or mask or use tools or power objects that represent a power animal by painting the animal on the tool or object.

5. **Other power allies.** As well as animals, plants and minerals can also serve as power spirits. These will be discussed later in the sections on Plants and Minerals.

SHAMANIC TOOLS

Tools are used in all types of rituals. They direct or store power, embody spirits, and can act as helpers for, or work independently of, you. The main tools a practitioner uses include ritual objects such as an altar, ritual items such as incense, sonic drivers such as a drum or rattle, and power objects such as talismans and amulets. You should be able to journey without tools if needed. A tool can also be used remotely by connecting to it energetically, or in journey. Tools can also exist in spiritual reality as well as physical reality.

All tools can contain other tools, and often include animal and plant parts, wood, metal or other objects. Tools are usually decorated with symbols relevant to their use or to the practitioner's symbology. Tools can also be associated with elements: incense and feathers with air, candles with fire, shells and containers with water, and crystals with earth. Wands are associated with air or fire. Vertical objects like candles are also symbols of the world tree.

Shamanic Tool Types

The main ritual objects are altars and shrines, costumes and masks, mirrors, ritual containers, and spirit representations like statues. Costumes or masks can hold power or spirits and help a practitioner transition to an altered state of consciousness. Mirrors are often used in divination rituals and may be attached to costumes to repel energy. Ritual containers such as bowls or cauldrons are used on altars and shrines, typically to make offerings. Statues and other representations of spirit are used on altars and shrines to facilitate spirit contact, to bring the power of a spirit into a ritual, or as a focus for offerings to that spirit.

Altars and shrines can contain other tools and objects. Altars are used to help create sacred space, provide a focal point for work, work with spirit, and anchor power. Shrines are used to honor and remember spirits or people, and are a place for solitude, remembering, and healing. Spirits may live in shrines. Altars tend to be indoors and shrines outdoors. Altars are more temporary and can be moved or retired, and they change over time with objects being substituted, perhaps to include seasonal offerings. Shrines are more permanent and static. You could have several altars and shrines, such as a main working altar and an ancestral altar or shrine.

The main ritual items used are incense and herbs, other plant products, shells, feathers, candles, and crystals. Incense and herbs are burnt to cleanse and purify sacred space, people, or objects, attract positive energy, and in healing. Other plant products include essential oils. Shells are used as containers, often to hold burning plant material in clearing rituals. Feathers, often combined in a fan, are used to move or align energy and in clearing. Candles are used in most rituals and as offerings. Crystals can be used in rituals and on altars.

Sonic drivers like drums, rattles, bells, singing bowls, whistles, and flutes are used to facilitate journeys. Frame drums are often used as they are easy to hold. Drums can be made with animal or synthetic skin. The former may need preparation depending on heat and humidity, and many people therefore use synthetic skins. Drumsticks are also tools and are sometimes used as rattles if they have metal attachments. Rattles are usually made from seeds or pebbles in a gourd or animal-hide container with a handle made from wood or horn. Bells may be used in rituals or on tools such as costumes. Whistles and flutes can be used to call spirits.

Divination tools include scrying objects, object collections that are thrown, and objects such as cards, runes, and pendulums. Scrying objects include mirrors (typically black), crystals, or by bringing elements into a ritual, such as a candle flame or the surface of water in a container.

Stick tools include wands, staffs, prayer sticks, and shaman trees. Wands have a round end to collect energy and a pointed end to focus it. A crystal is often used for a wand's tip. A prayer stick falls from a tree into the same or another tree without touching the ground. The big end determines its direction. They are used in ceremony, typically decorated and placed in the relevant direction. Shaman trees are trees decorated with cloth strips used to make offerings, express gratitude, honor or provide a home for spirits, or carry prayers to spirit. They are often at power places like crossroads and may have unusual features like multiple trunks.

Power objects are channels and stores for energy. The main power objects are talismans, amulets, charms, crystals, mandalas, prayer beads, and shields. Talismans are used to bring things to us; amulets are used to keep things away from us. Charms attract good luck, and thus are a form of talisman. Mandalas are used for healing or as a portal to bring energy into a ritual or access spiritual reality. Prayer beads are used to focus or count prayers, assisting in changing consciousness, or grounding. They may be worn on clothing. A shield attracts or repels energy and breaks energy blocks. It is usually made of skin over a hoop.

Other tools include art, song, dance, medicine bundles, dream tools, and containers. Art can act as a portal or house spirit and can be added to tools. Songs are given by spirit and are used to enter a trance, carry power, call spirit, or in healing. Dance deepens trance and facilitates spirit connection and can be used to honor power animals by incorporating their movements. A medicine bundle contains objects and helps connect to, represent, or embody spirit, and it can offer protection, heal, or act for a practitioner. Dream catchers keep unwanted dreams away; dream makers serve to attract wanted dreams. Object containers include bags, chests, and boxes used to store tools, objects, and ritual items. They can be part of an altar.

Making Shamanic Tools

Tools and materials can be bought, gifted, found in nature, or made. Making tools lets you forge a deep relationship with them. When making a tool you can journey to an archetypal spirit of that type of tool and to the individual spirit of the tool to find out what it will be used for, and how to make, decorate, dedicate, consecrate, activate, empower, and use it. If you are gifted or purchase a tool, you journey to its spirit to find out how to consecrate and use it.

Having journeyed to tool spirits, you can then gather or purchase objects to be used in making a tool. Construct and decorate the tool as you have been guided. This may be simple or can involve elaborate work with wood, metal, and animal skins. For the latter, it is often best to attend a specialist workshop to learn how to do this properly and safely.

Decoration can include painting a tool or adding animal, plant, mineral or metal components, or other objects. Often a tool such as a drum is decorated with symbols of power animals or helping spirits, or more abstract symbols that have deep personal meaning to you.

Consecration cleanses a tool, dedicates it for its purpose, and empowers it. Place the tool on an altar or cloth, clear it as you clear sacred space, and empower it. Merge with a tool spirit and transfer power into the tool as you are guided with an intention it is empowered for its use. This could involve blowing power into the tool or using your hands to pass power into it. The ritual used to consecrate a tool does not need to be elaborate. It can just involve invoking relevant spirits, lighting a candle, stating the purpose, and thanking spirit.

Tools like drums are awakened by using them while stating an intention for them and calling power into them. Tools like wands or crystals can be are programmed for a purpose. The handle of tools like wands can be wrapped with a material like leather to insulate the tool from your energy. Perform any other work required as advised by spirit.

Making an altar or shrine involves deciding an organizing principle, where and when to build it, what materials it is made of, and what objects to put on it. An organizing principle could include associating areas of the altar or shrine with directions and elements (four areas); having areas devoted to the upper, middle and lower worlds, or to past, present, and future (three areas).

When deciding where to place an altar or shrine consider direction, height, and privacy. Some traditions place it in a specific direction. Make an altar or shrine at standing or knee height if you intend to stand or sit in front of it. It can be on the floor but may not be easy to work with. If you do not want to advertise the object's use, or want to avoid people knocking into it, put it in a private space. You can also disguise an altar or shrine. Altars can be on a table, box, or flat surface. Shrines can be located indoors, in a garden or in nature. Trees and flat rocks make good natural altars and help ground energy.

An altar or shrine can be built at a specific time, like a moon phase. Altars used to bring something into your life should be built when the moon is waxing or at the full moon; those used to remove something from your life or observe an ending should be built while the moon is waning. A good time to build an altar for a new start is at the new moon.

Use materials that reflect the altar or shrine's intention and that are meaningful to you. Natural materials direct and anchor energy and reinforce connection with nature. Outdoor altars or shrines can be made with stacked stones or spirals/circles made of stones or wood. A common elemental altar used at entrances is a candle floating in a bowl of water. Altars and shrines should be solid. An enclosed space or drawer can be used to store ritual items that will be used on the altar or shrine during ceremonies and rituals. Altars may be carried, the contents housed in a box or cloth that can serve as the surface on which objects are placed.

On altars and shrines we place representations of spirits or people, symbols, candles, incense, bowls, and items from nature like feathers or stones. Symbols are often used. In ceremonies and rituals, we often use a cloth, tools like a wand and power objects on altars. For shrines the focus is more on offerings.

For a first altar, you can simply use a single candle placed in the center of a cloth or area. Items can be added later as relevant. In this way, your altar evolves as you use it, and your relationship with it grows stronger as its components mirror your own spiritual development.

A talisman is used to attract a quality, an amulet to protect or drive away, and a charm to attract good luck. Some combine several functions. Talismans and amulets are made from natural and artificial materials and may just be an object like a picture or a crystal. Objects, symbols and shapes with attributes relevant to the tool's intention may be placed or inscribed on talismans, amulets, and charms.

These tools are dedicated to the person who will use them when they are made. Spirits may live in talismans and amulets. A talisman, amulet or charm is made by the person who will use it or handled as little as possible if made for another.

Note that you can make tools in spiritual reality while you are journeying, as well as in physical reality. This tool stays in spiritual reality, perhaps at your sacred place or seat of power until you want to use it, or you can call it to you to accompany you in a journey. Spiritual reality tools can also work together with physical reality tools. For example, you can intend that a spiritual reality tool passes power to a physical reality tool which you use in physical reality.

Tools are typically stored in a container or covered when not in use.

Working with Shamanic Tools

Tools should be cleared before use, typically after you clear sacred space, and after use. A tool can be re-consecrated if it has not been used for a while. Tools should not be handled by others to avoid energy pollution or discharge. You can set an intention that a tool is only effective if used by you or a named person. If tools are handled by others they may need to be cleansed. Tools may be prepared for use by including them in ceremonies, where they act as spectators and become accustomed to their destined role as helpers.

When you make or consecrate and empower tools, you invest them with spiritual power. When used over time, they attract and hold more power, and their influence and effectiveness increases. This also helps your own development. Most tools can be used for clearing, healing, and divination. Some tools can act for a practitioner and heal without the practitioner being involved. Tools you handle are usually held in your dominant hand (the one you write with).

Altars should be worked with regularly. A morning ceremony can be held at an altar to start the day. This can simply involve lighting a candle, burning incense, making a small offering to spirit, giving thanks, and asking for guidance. You can perform a similar evening ceremony to review the day, identify lessons, and set future intentions. Use new candles and fresh flowers where possible in such rituals.

Put altar tools and ritual items away when an altar is not being used and periodically clean it. An altar should be kept current. Be guided as to whether items should be removed or added. You may want to periodically dismantle and reconstruct an altar. Ancestral altars and shrines are dealt with in the section on *Ancestral Healing*.

Putting on a costume or mask signals that you will be working with spirit, deepens trance, and may initiate merging or shape-shifting. A mask also breaks up your visual field, also facilitating a trance state, and may serve to disguise a practitioner from spirits.

Drums are held using strings or a frame at the back and struck with a beater. The sound depends how and where you hit it. Volume increases toward the center, where sound is deep and full, and is higher and hollower as you move toward the rim. A balance is to hit it a third of the way in from the rim. For journeying use a steady beat with no accents (emphasis on a beat). To clear space, intend a drum pushes energy out; for healing, intend it brings it in.

Wands are used to extract or direct energy. They can be used in healing to scan a person's body for energy blocks or misplaced energy, to extract energy (with the tip pointing away from them), empower a person (with the tip pointing toward them), or to smooth their energy. Like a wand, a feather also has a receptor (rounded) end and a tip (pointed) end. You can use it as we do a wand to clear, insert, or smooth energy.

Talismans may be worn, carried or kept close. A talisman should be charged with power when the moon is waxing. Amulets protect individuals, families, homes, vehicles, etc. Amulets are often worn close to the body, typically as a necklace or pendant, or can be placed on the edge of a property. Knots are sometimes used in amulets as they are believed to be able to catch spirits. An amulet should be charged with power when the moon is waning. Charms can be written, spoken or sung, or be objects. Charms do not need to be visible but can be carried in a bag or worn under clothing.

If a tool must be retired, deconsecrate it as guided before dismantling or disposing of it.

Key Ritual: Journey to the Spirit of the Drum

The intention is to journey to the spirit of the drum to introduce yourself to it and find out how you will work with it.

> *Sue*
>
> In spirit, the drum had a bluey-green shimmery look to it. It comes alive and is more like water or an energy form, it was not solid. The first thing that came was that it needs to be sprinkled with water. To consecrate it, I will take it down to the sea and just rinse it through the water and then sit with a fire, which may just be a candle, and sit by the water's edge and play the drum until I know when to stop.
>
> When I asked how to use it for healing, it was about drawing down the elements. I am to play it at the beginning of

a session to connect people to spirit multi-dimensionally and use it to clear space. I saw pictures of a healing starting and everything was coming through the drum and blowing away energy, there was so much coming through. I use it to get people to go into a trance and relax and then draw down and use the elements as I am guided to do that.

The divination was to play the drum and then I would basically move into the drum and journey into a cave. I traveled into a cave and there is a pool, a divination pool. I am to take questions and will see answers play out in the pool. I was not expecting that; I thought it would be something different. I asked a simple question about my studies and whether I was going to pass. I saw myself in the water wearing a gown, like I was watching it on TV. I took that to mean I would pass.

When I asked how else I would work with it, I kept seeing myself walking and taking my drum with me and playing the drum. It was like it became an extension of me. If I am in need of anything, I am to play the drum. I am also to take it with me and just share the energy. It will be powerful when I am out, not powerful for me particularly just a powerful healing of some kind. I saw myself sitting on my roof playing it, I saw myself walking through the trees and out through nature, sometime with people and sometimes without people, sometimes in a room with people. I was sitting there playing the drum in the middle of everybody.

How to Do the Key Ritual

You can choose to work with an archetypal spirit, in this case the spirit of all drums, or to work with the individual spirit specific to your drum. Here you work with the specific spirit of your drum to find out what purposes the tool will be used for. The intention is to journey to the spirit of the drum to introduce yourself to it, to ask how you will acquire, decorate and consecrate your drum, and find out how to work with it, including for healing and divination.

Ask if it has any other general advice for how you will work with it. You can also ask if there is anything else the drum would like you to do for it, such as decorating it, or making some sort of offering to it. You can make offerings to spirit in journey by manifesting something they would like, or they ask for, or that you are guided to give. You can also make offerings at a physical reality altar. Take the same approach for working with other shamanic tools.

Other Rituals

Other rituals that you can perform include: journey to learn to make and use a physical reality altar or shrine, journey to learn how to make and use a spiritual reality altar or shrine; journey to the archetypal amulet, journey to the spirit of an amulet, journey to the archetypal talisman, and journey to the spirit of a talisman.

You can also journey to learn how to make a costume or mask to represent one of your spirits, or journey to learn how to design, make and consecrate other tools such as a staff.

Journey to Construct and Use a Physical Reality Altar or Shrine

The intention is to journey to learn how to build and use a physical reality altar or shrine.

Lilian

My altar needs to be simple. Where I have it is fine, but I need to redo it. I am to start with four stones at the corners and a candle in the middle. The stones should be simple, not crystals. I have been collecting stones and I am to find from my collection what I am to use on the altar. I am to put away all the other stuff that is on the altar. I can have some flowers or crystals later. I am to set an appointment at eight every night with spirit. I am to project myself into spiritual reality and walk around a fire in a spiral. They will meet me there.

Journey on How to Make and Use a Spiritual Reality Altar or Shrine

The intention is to journey to learn how to construct and use a spiritual reality altar or shrine. Find out about any relationship between your spiritual and physical reality altars or shrines.

James

> I went to the tree in my sacred place and it had expanded
> everywhere up and down. It seemed a good meditation
> image to think of would be that with me in the middle.
> I imagine a flame that burns and expands everywhere.
> Then I was back with the Aborigines and one of them put
> a stone between my eyes. My spiritual altar is a tree that I
> am inside that expanded everywhere, with flame that melts
> everything into one.

Journey to the Archetypal Amulet

The intention is to journey to an archetypal spirit to get advice on how to work with amulets.

Sue

> I was moving a lot. I saw ceremony with fire, dancing and
> noise. I saw dragons, unicorns and snakes dancing. Every-
> thing was full of color, energy and movement. I asked how
> I could work with an amulet and it was through song.

Journey to the Spirit of an Amulet

The intention is to journey to the spirit of an amulet to find out how to work with it.

Sue

> I will walk in nature to find a stone, make marks in it,
> put it in fire and leave it overnight. I am to have water
> and sing while it is in the fire. It will be placed outside the
> front door. There is a dip in the top where I can add things
> like crystals, seeds, flowers or stick. I am to be aware of
> and interact with it each time I pass it. The intention is to
> protect, it is like a guardian to stop things coming in that
> shouldn't.

Journey to the Archetypal Talisman

The intention it to journey to an archetypal spirit to get advice on how to work with talismans.

Ryan

The talisman attracts things to me. It is also a symbol of what I want to attract. You have to know what you will do with energy you attract. A website is a talisman as you are attracting people, so you need to put thought into what you are trying to attract.

Lisa

Spirit was very clear. It said to be very clear about what you want to invite or attract to you, sit down and work out what you want to attract. It has to be for a higher purpose and for your development. Once you identify what you want to attract, work out what symbolises that; ask spirit to give you the symbol that will attract that and then create a form from that: a mandala, a picture, a Zen garden, a tapestry, a weaving of different colors, etc. Ask spirit to imbue it with intention and power. You have to check up on it regularly to see that is still current, still relevant, and needs recharging.

Journey to the Spirit of a Talisman

The intention is to journey to the spirit of a talisman to find out how to work with it.

Ryan

My talisman is a website (and can be a business card). It has writing of things I want to attract. The website attracts clients I want. It can be empowered by journeying to the website spirit or by passing power into the screen.

Lisa

I went to the upper world. My guide first asked what I want to attract. I said I would like to attract more energy into the clinic. She said I have to use symbols that consciously bring in that kind of energy. If I want the word to spread, I have to create a picture of a ripple, energy moving, an echo, etc. Bring things like a mandala or a vessel containing things that will bring in that kind of energy.

Pro Tips

The following tips are provided:

1. **Avoid tool collections.** Do not acquire objects and not use them or clutter altars with objects and tools. Use only tools you really need and try to keep an altar simple.

2. **Appropriation.** Some tools are culture-specific and should not be used outside that context, e.g., you should not use a Native American pipe unless you are a pipe carrier.

3. **Tool acquisition.** It is better to make your tools, or receive them as gifts, rather than buy them. If you buy tools, do so from ethical suppliers.

4. **Tool manufacture.** When we make tools, we put our energy into them. Make sure you understand the correspondences of all items and materials used to make tools.

5. **Gifts.** You may want to place a gift on your altar to endow it with positive energy.

ELEMENTS, DIRECTIONS, AND CYCLES

You work with elements to balance their energy in yourself and others. Across cultures there is a belief in four spirit powers associated with cardinal directions. You work with directions to align yourself with them. Elements and directions are typically called in at the start of ceremonies to bring their power to rituals. You also work with the correspondences between ritual components like elements and directions, and the associations that these components have. For example, the element air is associated with the direction east, both of which are associated with creativity. Another component of all spiritual work is observing and working with natural cycles, especially the solar and lunar cycles.

Elements and Directions

Different element systems are used in different cultures. Western traditions use the four-element system of air, fire, water, and earth. Sometimes a fifth element is added (Spirit). The Chinese elemental system comprises five elements: fire, water, earth, metal, and wood. Some traditions use three element systems with air omitted, and in some traditions, wind replaces air. These systems are different ways of understanding the world and are all effective.

Different conventions exist for numbers of directions, from four cardinal directions, to six if we add above and below, or seven if we also add the center. Some traditions work with an eight-direction system comprising the cardinal and cross-quarter directions, or more complex systems. Directions are represented in cross-cultural symbols like the encircled cross, with the power of the four directions implied and accessed whenever a crossed circle is drawn.

Elements and directions can be represented on altars, which should be simple, as well as being invoked in ceremony, and you can make and tend elemental and directional altars and shrines. If you do this as a group, it brings these energies into relationship with the group. You can also use elements and directions in rituals and work with elemental or directional spirits.

If you lack the influence of an element, you can work with a spirit associated with it as well as the element itself. You can also work with elements and directions collectively.

Some ideas for elemental rituals:

1. **Air.** Healing by standing in a wind to remove illness; divination by looking at clouds.

2. **Fire.** Healing by placing a symbol of illness in a fire; divination by looking into flames.

3. **Water.** Healing by washing away illness; divination by looking at water surface.

4. **Earth.** Healing by burying a symbol of illness; divination by casting stones.

You can also work with the winds, individually or collectively. Winds do not just represent the element air but are also associated with individual directions.

Correspondences and Associations

Things like elements, directions, herbs, crystals and colors have *correspondences* between them, often published in correspondence tables. Typical element correspondences are:

- Air is associated with the east, the color yellow, dawn, and spring.

- Fire is associated with the south, the color red, midday, and summer.

- Water is associated with the west, the color blue, dusk, and autumn.

- Earth is associated with the north, the color black, midnight, and winter.

- Spirit is associated with the center, the color green, timelessness and eternity.

As well as correspondences, elements and directions have *associations*: keywords used to determine an element and/or direction to work with for a specific intention. Like symbology, this can be personal, and you can determine your own associations. Some examples:

- **Air/East:** Beginnings, communication, creativity, inspiration, intellect, vision

- **Fire/South:** Courage, leadership, power, purification, success, transformation

- **Water/West:** Dreams, emotions, psychic abilities, purification, reflection, sleep

- **Earth/North:** Abundance, death and rebirth, fertility, grounding, wealth

Cycles

Many cycles in nature affect us, especially the lunar and solar cycles that cause tides and seasons and affect other natural cycles and our bodies. There are also cycles in spiritual reality, and between spiritual reality and physical reality. Understanding cycles allows us to reconnect with natural rhythms and integrate their energy into our lives and rituals. The main physical reality cycles and their timings are:

1. **Astronomical cycles.** These include earth's rotation on its axis each day, moon's orbit of Earth (lunar cycle) every twenty-nine days and Earth's orbit of the sun (solar cycle) each year.

2. **Biological cycles.** These include REM sleep cycles of about ninety minutes, biorhythms which have a twenty-three to thirty-three-day cycle, and seasonal or annual agricultural cycles.

3. **Climate cycles.** These include cycles that involved tides, seasons and monsoons, and longer-term cycles involved in climate change including ice ages and global warming.

The moon's gravitational pull on the earth causes tides and influences fluids, affecting bodily functions like ovulation and plant growth patterns. The moon influences our subconscious, emotions and feelings. The lunar cycle is defined by phases of the moon, which are the shape of the moon's sunlit portion, as seen from the earth, which changes as the moon orbits the earth and the relative positions of the moon, sun and earth change. There are four phases:

1. The new moon (or dark moon). The moon is not visible as it is between the earth and sun. Its influence is at its minimum. This is a time to rest or start new projects.

2. The waxing moon is when the illuminated surface increases, starting with a waxing crescent, and proceeding via the first quarter, a half moon, to the waxing gibbous. The moon's energy is increasing. This is a time to work on what we wish to attract.

3. The full moon is when the moon is on the opposite side of the earth to the sun and most light is reflected on it. The moon's influence is at

its maximum. This is a time to celebrate, complete things, and give thanks. The full moon can make us unbalanced.

4. The waning moon is when the illuminated surface decreases, starting with a waning gibbous, and proceeding via the third or last quarter, a half moon, to the waning crescent. The moon's energy is decreasing. This is a time to let go of things.

In the Northern Hemisphere, at temperate latitudes, when the moon is waxing, the left side is dark and the right side is light and growing; and when waning, the right side is dark and the left side is light and shrinking. In the Southern Hemisphere the opposite applies. At tropical latitudes, the moon's crescent is seen horizontally in the morning and evening.

There are special names for different full moons, which vary across cultures. The most well-known is the harvest moon, closest to the autumn equinox and the brightest moon. The moon rises later each night, helping farmers in harvest season by extending working hours.

We might expect at each new moon, the moon would cast a shadow on the earth causing a solar eclipse, and at every full moon the earth would cover the moon causing a lunar eclipse. This does not happen each month as the moon's orbital path around the earth is tilted from the earth-sun plane, so major eclipses of the sun or moon only occur about twice a year.

A blue moon is when a second full moon occurs in a month. As we do not follow a lunar calendar, a month does not equal one lunar orbit of the earth. Every thirty-three months or so, two full moons occur in a month, often before or after February (when a full moon may be skipped).

You should be aware of lunar and solar cycles, the seasons, their effect on you, and ritual timing implications. Note what happens at different moon phases to see if there are patterns or trends. You can cleanse and charge yourself and objects in the full moon's light. You can journey to the spirits of the moon and sun, or to lunar or solar deities.

Most locations experience seasons, the number varying by latitude. In temperate regions there are four (spring, summer, fall/autumn, and winter). Sometimes pre-spring, late summer or monsoon seasons are added. In hot regions there are two or three seasons, named dry, cool, hot, or wet. Seasons bring inner and outer changes and can affect you.

We can also work with cycles that occur in spiritual reality or between spiritual and physical reality. An example of the latter is the reincarnation cycle.

Seasonal Festivals

The earth's orbit about the sun is the basis of the solar cycle. Most cultures have an annual cycle of eight festivals, held at solstices, equinoxes and midpoints, which mark a season's start or middle. In Neopaganism, this cycle is called the *Wheel of the Year*. There are three fertility festivals between the winter and summer solstices, and three harvest festivals between the summer and winter solstices. The main motif is growth and the sun's "death" and "rebirth" at the winter solstice. Sacred sites are often aligned to events like sunrise on the summer solstice.

These festivals let you acknowledge transitions, the sun, earth, moon, and seasons. They are a time to look back and release things, or to look forward and plan the next cycle. In agricultural societies they were connected with planting and harvest, in hunting societies the hunting season, and in nomadic societies moving locations to follow animals. Solstice and equinox festivals represent symbolic renewal, of people, land and spirits. Examples of themes and shamanic rituals associated with festivals are as below:

1. **Winter Solstice.** This is held near the end of December in the Northern Hemisphere and the end of June in the Southern Hemisphere. The theme is rebirth and a new cycle; rituals include vision quests.

2. **First fertility festival.** This is held at the start of February in the Northern Hemisphere and the start of August in the Southern Hemisphere; the theme is purification and spring cleaning; rituals are concerned with light and candles.

3. **Second fertility festival (Spring Equinox).** This is held near the end of March in the Northern Hemisphere and end of September in the Southern Hemisphere. The theme is balance and renewal; rituals are concerned with fertility symbols like eggs.

4. **Third fertility festival.** This is held at the start of May in the Northern Hemisphere and the start of November in the Southern Hemisphere. The theme is sexual union. Rituals are concerned with fire and male symbols like poles.

5. **Summer Solstice.** This is held near the end of June in the Northern Hemisphere and the end of December in the Southern Hemisphere. The theme is growth and prosperity. Rituals are again concerned with fire and also with healing.

6. **First harvest festival.** This is held at the start of August in the Northern Hemisphere and the start of February in the Southern Hemisphere. The theme relates to the harvest of grain and fruits. Rituals are concerned with bread or corn figures.

7. **Second harvest festival (Autumn Equinox).** This is held toward the end of September in the Northern Hemisphere and the end of March in the Southern Hemisphere. The theme is thanksgiving. Rituals are concerned with releasing the past.

8. **Third harvest festival.** This is held at the end of October in the Northern Hemisphere and the end of April in the Southern Hemisphere. The theme is remembrance, and preparing for death of the Sun. This is a time to do divination and shadow work.

Key Ritual: Calling in the Directions and Elements

You can use this ritual when creating sacred space within a ceremony, to invoke directions and elemental powers into your ritual work before you call in your spirits. You can amend the previous ceremony guidelines to include this component.

The following is a basic invocation in the first person that includes direction correspondences and associations. Feel free to reword this as you are guided, to change the associations to fit a particular ritual that you want to perform, or to otherwise personalize it as you are guided.

> I call in the east, air, vision, illumination, and inspiration.
>
> I call in the south, fire, creativity, maturity, and manifestation.
>
> I call in the west, water, introspection, intuition, and psychic ability.
>
> I call in the north, earth, abundance, fertility, and rebirth.

I call in the above, the sky, sun, moon, and stars.

I call in the below, Mother Earth.

I call in the center, spirit.

I thank you all and ask you to bless and help in my work.

You could then call in other helping spirits as relevant for the ritual you are performing.

How to Do the Key Ritual

You can use the basic template provided above to construct your own invocation for the elements and directions, together with their relevant correspondences and associations. You can amend the basic approach to include other correspondences that you want to include for your personal practice. This could include one or more of the following:

1. Changing the elemental correspondence with the directions if you are working within a tradition that does this in a different way.

2. Adding or removing correspondences. For instance, some people associate power animals, spirits, archangels or deities with directions.

3. Substituting the associations suggested with your own.

You should be aware of cardinal directions at all times. You can check this with a compass or by seeing where the sun rises and sets.

When invoking a direction, you might extend a hand to the direction and draw it toward you as a welcome gesture. Start with a direction that feels appropriate (often north or east) and proceed clockwise. When working with a direction, some traditions state that we should face it. Others say that we should face away from it so that we are in alignment with the flow of its energy and not opposed to it. Work as you are guided.

Other Rituals

Other rituals that you can perform include: journey to find out how to make an elemental altar or shrine, journey to find out how to raise and use elemental power, journey to the spirit compass, journey to learn about the moon, journey to the seasons, journey to find out about individual cycles in our lives, and journey to learn about cycles between spiritual and physical reality.

You can also journey to the elements or directions, individually or collectively, to the sun, and to find out about seasonal affective disorder and how to heal this.

Journey to Find Out How to Make an Elemental Altar or Shrine

The intention is to journey to the element concerned to get their advice about making, using and tending an altar or shrine.

Ann

The water shrine will be by a river or sea. I was told not to be static and have fun with it. I will stack stones and consecrate it with six handfuls or coconuts of water from the sea or river. I will make shrines in different places where I go and tend them. I saw about twelve of them in different places; it seemed to be in different countries. They said it does not take long to make. It should be simple; have fun with it.

Journey to Find Out How to Raise and Use Elemental Power

The intention is to journey to get information on raising and using elemental power. We want to know what sort of intention we should use, how power is raised, and how we can use it.

Ryan

The intention should have a narrow focus or purpose, an altruistic motive, and needs to address an imbalance. To raise elemental power, we can bring in symbols of the elements like the candle. The more that we tend to these symbols, the greater the power we will be able to bring into a ceremony. The intention should be to raise the power for a specific purpose and make sure residual power is dissipated at the end.

Journey to the Spirit Compass

The intention is to journey to an archetypal spirit associated with the directions to get advice about working with directions. Here this spirit is referred to as the spirit compass. If you just intend to be taken to this spirit to learn about directions, you will meet an appropriate spirit.

Ann

> I journeyed to the lower world and was told that the directions have depth in the attributes we associate with them. We should not just learn words but learn the vibrations underneath those to understand what we work with when we call in the directions. The vibrations give us the power for action. We should learn to invoke the appropriate direction based on its energetic characteristics and what we want to do in ceremony and ritual. I was told to work with north as I am not grounded.

Journey to Learn about the Moon

The intention is to journey to the moon to find out how its cycles affect you.

Ann

> My present work would be greatly enhanced by working with the moon. At the new moon I should set intentions in meditation, then follow guidance and work over the next moon or three moons. At the full moon I go outside, cup my hands and put water in them. I stand and hold my hands straight up with to infuse water with moonlight and drink it. On the twenty-third day of the cycle, there is a day of reflection. I am powerful when I sit before the moon.

Journey to the Seasons

The intention is to journey to the seasons to find out how they affect us.

Lilian

> I am at my best and strongest when it is winter and cold. In summer it is important for me to lie low and to stay

close to the ground (I take this to mean grounded). For short projects think in terms of moon cycles, but for longer projects think in terms of a year.

Journey to Find Out about Individual Cycles in Our Lives

The intention is to journey to find out what cycles you are stuck in and how to break free from them, or positive cycles that would benefit you and how to strengthen or create them.

Lilian

My life tends to move in eight-year cycles, which is true; significant things tend to happen then. My mental cycle is very active when it comes to strong planning and having ideas, but it is completely out of whack with my physical cycle. I need to work with my first three chakras and learn how to put things into action. Emotions are not a cycle but something that weaves into the others.

Journey to Learn about Cycles Between Spiritual and Physical Reality

The intention is to journey to understand cycles that involve both physical and spiritual reality.

Ryan

I did reincarnation. Brigid explained it with a candle. A candlelight burns. The flame is the soul. As it goes out, you can transfer that flame to another candle and the experience starts again. It is still the same soul, just experiencing life differently.

Pro Tips

The following tips are provided:

1. **Symbols.** You can bring elements and directions into your life via symbols on an altar.

2. **Visualisation.** A key to working with elements is being able to strongly visualize them. The better you can do this, the more effective your work will be.

3. **Balance.** If you work with an element more than others, we develop an excess of its energy. You should work with all of the elements, which helps to achieve balance.

4. **True self.** Elements are true to their nature and help us to connect to our true selves.

5. **Approach to cycles.** We should see cycles as part of our lives rather than just conducting ceremonies on special occasions. We should be aware that these cycles are part of a larger context and interact with each other.

DIVINATION

Divination is a way to gain knowledge and insight by using rituals to reveal hidden information and find answers. It has been, and continues to be, practiced in all cultures. For traditional peoples, divination was used for purposes including finding food sources. Divination is often done as an intentional ritual but can also occur spontaneously during other work.

Shamanic divination involves obtaining information from spirits, or interpretation of patterns or sensory experiences. This includes using journeys or dreams to ask spirit questions, spirit merging, channeling, casting and reading objects, scrying, or interpreting shamanic tool movements. As with journeys and dreams, divination often involves symbol interpretation.

The main reasons for doing divination are:

1. To confirm a ceremony or ritual should be performed.

2. To find out if a person is ill, diagnose the illness, or confirm healing needed.

3. To access hidden or distant information, including finding things that are lost.

4. To get answers or input to decisions, such as if a building should be built in a location.

5. To predict or get advice about the future or learn things about the past or past lives.

One common classification of divination methods is the following:

1. **Omens.** Noticing unusual or important events like natural phenomena.

2. **Augury.** Interpreting signs or patterns in nature, such as bird flight or cloud patterns.

3. **Scrying.** Interpretation by gazing at objects like a crystal, mirror, candle, or water.

4. **Direct methods.** Getting information directly from a spirit in journey, dream or vision, or by channelling information from a spirit in the same way a medium works.

5. **Indirect methods.** Using a single object, for instance to select an answer from a list.

6. **Sortilege.** This involves throwing (casting) objects like sticks or stones on a surface. Divination is via meanings assigned to objects based on where and how they land.

In practice, multiple methods can be used at the same time. A practitioner may cast objects to get an answer to a question, interpret the resulting patterns made by the objects, and also clarify specific aspects or follow-up questions via direct communication with a spirit.

With some forms of divination, you may be able change a predicted outcome by making a change in spiritual or physical reality. For example, changing the pattern of objects cast in a sortilege divination to reflect a preferred outcome with an intention that this is manifested.

Omens

Divination via omens involves obtaining information from the natural world by interpretation of signs or unusual events. Omens may be good or bad depending on their interpretation; the same omen may be interpreted differently by different people or cultures. Other omens include the same thing happening multiple times such as seeing repeated numbers or symbols.

Astronomical events like meteors, comets, eclipses, full moons, or planetary conjunctions are often omens. Eclipses and comets are considered omens of significant events. Weather events often act as omens with weather patterns being important to agricultural societies.

Animal presence is often interpreted as an omen, especially when they are in unusual locations. Birds are especially important, with all birds being regarded as messengers, and the presence of specific species having different meanings and interpretations.

Good omens include doves, cuckoos, robins, swallows, wrens, bees, ladybirds, sheep, goats, piebald horses, and hedgehogs. Bad omens include ravens and crows, owls, gulls, kingfishers, sparrows, bats, wasps, pigs, a hare crossing your path, and dogs howling at the moon.

Seeing a single magpie is a bad omen but two is a good omen. Squirrels are a good omen, but squirrels gathering nuts early is a sign of a bad winter. A cat leaving your house is a bad omen. White or brown mice are a good omen but gray ones a bad omen. White rats are good omens but black ones bad. Ants are a good omen but being bitten by one is bad. Spiders are a good omen if they are on your body. Crickets are a good omen but one leaving a garden a bad omen.

When in nature, note what you see and experience, especially unusual events. You may well receive signs if you are facing a key life decision. Omens grab your attention, feel meaningful, and affect you strongly and make you feel that there is a hidden meaning being conveyed to you. Try to interpret a meaning and, if you feel that you have received guidance from spirit, offer thanks for this and note the event and see what happens soon afterward.

Augury

Augury is a type of omen-based divination where patterns in nature are used, in particular the behavior of birds and animals, and examination of body parts. Techniques include: forecasting the weather by interpreting bird cries; foretelling the future by the croaking of frogs or other animal noises; staring at the sky when it is full of clouds, searching for an answer to a question; and using animal bones or other body parts, with images being detected in the parts.

Scrying

The word *scrying* means to reveal or to perceive. A scryer will typically gaze at one of the following to perform divination: water (especially the reflection of the sun or moon on a water surface), fire or a candle flame (or smoke patterns from a fire), a mirror (usually a dark mirror, often used in conjunction with a candle), or a crystal or a crystal ball (especially a clear quartz one).

To scry, you allow your vision to become unfocused and clear your mind, which should put you into a light trance. Spirit can communicate using the element or object. You may see images, shapes, symbols, shapes, or shadows, interpreting these in relation to a question. You may also discern information by sound, such as the crackling of logs in a fire.

Direct Methods

These can be used to confirm a need for divination, verify results, or get clarification. You get information directly from spirit, with answers typically received as messages, images, or symbols which you interpret. The following methods are used: journeying to a spirit to ask a question (or meeting the spirit in a dream or vision), channeling information from a spirit in physical reality, merging with a helping spirit in physical reality, or using your or another person's energy body to discern meaning (or the truth).

You can journey to one of your own or another person's helping spirit or another spirit. A classical form of this is using the Sun to show us a location on a map with a sunbeam that identifies where something is or where an event will occur. You can also use the moon in an analogous way or infer answers from the moon's appearance.

A diagnostic journey to detect the presence of illness is the tunnel journey where you journey into a person's body in the middle world, entering their head and moving down to the feet to scan for signs of illness. Healing can also be performed in such a journey. You can also see into another person's energy body to diagnose illness and healing needed.

In channeling or merging, you ask a question and receive a response. An advantage of this technique is that you remain in a conscious state, which allows interaction and follow-up questions if you are doing work for another person. When doing this, especially publicly, the hardest thing for new practitioners is to start talking. As soon as you do it gets easier. You can close your eyes if you find this helps this practice.

You can use your energy body to discern an answer, or the truth, with a yes/no answer. One way to do this is to center and ground, ask to be shown what a "yes" answer feels like, or make a true statement, and notice the effect in your energy body. Then ask to be shown what a "no" answer feels like, or make a false statement, and see if you can detect a difference. You can then use this approach in practice. A common sign of a falsehood or "no" answer is a tense feeling or an ache in the region of a chakra, often the second chakra.

Indirect Methods

Indirect divination methods involve the use of an object, typically a tool, to focus your intention, get information or diagnose illness. This is done by interpreting tool movements or weight changes. Tools provide focus. The following are examples of using single objects:

- **Drum beaters.** Beaters with differently shaped sides can be thrown in the air and the side that lands upward used to infer the answer to a yes/no question. Beaters can also be thrown or spun on the ground to select a person from a group, or an option from a choice, with reference to the direction that the drum beater head points to.

- **Feathers.** A feather can be used as a diagnostic tool, the movement of the feather, or a sensation, confirming the location of illness or stuck energy. Feathers are also hung from a staff to indicate presence of spirits or the direction they come from.

- **Hand.** A hand can be used as a diagnostic tool in a similar manner to that for feathers. A hand may also be moved or shaken, as you are guided, when performing such divination, with changes in the hand or a finger movement providing the diagnosis. You can also perform diagnosis by detecting temperature fluctuations.

- **Held objects.** We can infer answers from changes in apparent weight of an object; it will feel lighter or heavier when a right answer is spoken, which can be used to confirm the correct option from a list of choices. You must determine the significance of different answers in the same way as the energy body method.

- **Pendulum.** An object can be hung on a thread or chain and its movement used to infer an answer. Test questions with known answers determine movement meanings.

- **Drum or rattle.** A drum, rattle or similar instrument can be moved over a person with a change in its noise or movement providing a diagnosis.

- **Drum.** The surface of a drum can be painted with symbols or images. The drum is laid down, an indicator like a pointer placed on top, and the drum beaten so that the pointer moves on to, or points to, a symbol or image that provides the answer.

- **Rocks.** A practitioner gets an answer by focusing on a rock allowing images, words, symbols or feelings to form. Each rock face represents a different aspect of the question and answer. Input obtained is combined into an overall answer.

- **Animal bones.** Animal parts like shoulder blades were traditionally used, often blackened in a fire. The apparent weight change of a held bone could indicate the answer to a question, a lighter (or heavier) weight signifying a positive response or a preferred answer from a list that is read out while the practitioner holds the bone.

- **Passing objects over a person.** A number of different techniques use objects passed over a person's body to infer information about them, especially health. This includes passing eggs over a person and interpreting the egg's condition or passing a candle over a person and interpreting the flame color, movement, or shape.

Sortilege

This involves casting objects like stones on a surface. Divination is via meanings assigned to objects based on where and how they land. You can take journeys to confirm how objects are to be used and get information about their meanings. Objects are cast, and divination made by interpreting individual objects and their relationship to each other.

You can also use objects to change the future. Several objects are cast to answer a question. The cluster of objects represents a future state, which can be changed by changing the pattern of the objects. You can remove, add or move individual objects to affect the outcome.

We will refer to the area used to cast objects and perform divination rituals as a *canvas* (even if no cloth is used). The following are examples of divination canvas layouts:

1. **Two zones.** A canvas is divided into two areas, e.g., upper and lower or left and right. One interpretation used with canvas is positive

versus negative e.g., if an object is cast in the upper zone it is interpreted positively and if in the lower zone negatively.

2. **Three zones.** A canvas is divided into three areas, e.g., left, middle and right. One motif used is past, present and future e.g., an object cast in the left zone relates to the past, one in the middle the present, and one in the right the future.

3. **Four zones.** A canvas is divided into four areas, which relate to e.g., directions, elements, energy bodies (physical, emotional, mental and spiritual), or body parts.

4. **Wheel.** A canvas is divided into multiple zones corresponding to medicine wheel directions or other attributes. A meaning is assigned to each wheel segment.

When using a canvas, be clear about whose perspective is taken in interpreting zones. If a left, middle and right zone canvas is used is this from a practitioner's or another person's perspective (assuming they sit opposite each other)? If you sit side by side, this issue is avoided.

A subset or all the objects are held by a person in one or both hands. They focus on a question and the objects are cast on the canvas. The meaning of one or more objects cast is inferred in relation to the canvas zone it falls on, and its relationship to other objects.

What does it mean if an object falls outside the canvas? It could be that it is less significant or that it has no bearing on the subject. You could decide that an object that lands off the canvas is not used in the divination. If an object falls on the boundary between two or more zones, we could use the meaning of all relevant zones to arrive at a meaning for that object. We can also use our intuition, ask for guidance, or perform further divination when this occurs.

Interpret each piece in terms of its individual meaning and position on the canvas. Finally offer a summation based on the previous analysis of the individual objects.

Key Ritual: Channeling from and/or Merging with a Spirit

The intention is to connect to spirit to get information. This is done publicly speaking out loud if you are trying to get information for another person.

Maya

Okay, so I am seeing a sort of like angelic figure and its standing on a precipice like a cliff, but it is the edge of the universe, so it's not necessarily like a bad thing. I feel there is a choice to go forward or to come back and that the angel wants to go forward. It's a really scary choice because maybe you have to fly, and it's like do you take this step into the unknown and to go into this limitless possibility, or are you staying where you're comfortable and know there's hard earth beneath you rather than spreading your wings and soaring into whatever it is that... Oh, you flew!

We're flying in the stars right now, hang on. Okay, so you ended up in like a beautiful forest area and there is a babbling brook. If you take whatever this journey is, you will land in a beautiful place, but the point is it is on solid ground, and it will be very different from the ground you were on. This is very abundant, its natural, it's gorgeous, you have the earth and the water and the air, whereas previously it was kind of like you were at the end of whatever. It was dark and it was gray and there wasn't a lot of light there.

Where you ended there is a lot of beauty and grace, grace is the word that just came into my head. Abundance, grace and beauty where you are going. So, it's like not a literal place though. You walked through the water, and I interpret that this place is also going to help you let go of what you were holding onto before, a sort of baptism if you will. You are crossing over to the next shore and allowing the water to take the stuff you are holding onto; you are allowing that to wash away. You are happy.

How to Do the Key Ritual

Decide if you are going to ask a question or just be open to receiving information. This could be from one of your spirits or another spirit. You could also merge with one of your spirits, which may make it easier to receive information. Drop your attention from your head to your heart and be open to receive communication. The most difficult thing is to start talking.

You may get symbols, images or words. For non-verbal communication, interpret the meaning that the symbols or images you receive mean to you. Do not be concerned where it is coming from as long as it feels authentic. Do not interpret what is given or filter the message. If you relay information and you or another person ask another question, then intend to answer that as well and continue a dialogue until a natural break is reached, the question has been fully explored, or next steps have been identified.

Other Rituals

Other rituals that you can perform include: journey to a divination spirit, journey to get a divination from spirit, scrying using a crystal, journey to perform divination by the sun, and journey to perform divination by the moon.

You can also scry using fire or water or try single or multiple object divination.

Journey to a Divination Spirit

The intention is to journey to a specialist divination spirit to get general advice on divination.

> #### Salina
> I met a Scottish lady, ginger haired with a helmet. I asked her for advice and the answer that came back was that divination is the art of seeing beyond what we call reality. In my case it is deciphering signs, hunches, dreams, messages I can get from dreams, gut feelings, messages that you get in your body or in meditation.

Journey to Get a Divination from Spirit

The intention is to journey to spirit to get an answer to a question that you or another person would like an answer to, or to get a general divination for the person.

> #### Lucie
> It is the first time it happened to me, but I flew with my Raven and we were the size of a bee, both of us. So, we fly into a huge field full of purple flowers and it's beautiful.

I saw you, slightly bigger than a fairy with those wings like a *Peter Pan* fairy, with colors like green and very shiny wings. There is a very bright sun, and when the sun goes down and the night comes, you grow bigger, much bigger, like normal size.

Then you have these dark clothes with signs like stars on the back. Then you fly and collect a message. All the flowers they kind of give away some small lights, and these purple lights carry a message. It is not really talking; you receive or collect that message. The flowers are talking to you like that. I asked what does it mean? It is something to do with magic, the only word that came was "magic." It is to do with the night and those purple flowers.

Scrying Using a Crystal

Here we work with a crystal, preferably a clear quartz crystal. Gaze into the crystal and intend that an answer to a question is communicated from spirit.

Maya

I'm not sure I like it. I saw this face. I asked who the face was, and they said, "Your husband." Not only do I not want him to look like that, but I am not in the market for one. Then there was another face and I said, "Who's that?" and they said, "Your son." The river appeared. It pinpointed a piece of land I would like to buy but cannot afford.

Then there was an angry face and I said, "Who is this?" and they said it was my neighbor. I asked why they were showing my neighbour and they said, "He is angry, but he will help you a lot, don't be put off by his anger." Then I saw a baby puppy; she is so cute. That was not what I expected.

Journey to Perform Divination by the Sun

This is a divination journey whose intention is to find the location of a person, object, or place where an event will occur. The main information given is the location. Intend to journey to a place where you can visualise or sense being in an open landscape.

Thinking of the question, ask the sun to show you the location of what you are searching for. One sunbeam will shine brightly or in another way attract your attention. Follow this beam (if necessary, traveling over the landscape) until the beam touches the ground, which is the location. When you recognise the location and can match it to a place in physical reality, return from the journey.

Ann

Everything was really clear, crystal clear, and surprisingly clear. I asked to be taken to a location that would be my next step, whatever format that took. This ray of sunshine came in and pointed to Italy, the south side. I was there in that area with a group of people in the sea, laughing and shouting.

Then I came out and was in the street on the sidewalk at a little round table with a man I do not know, and we were doing books, accounts for a course that we were running. I was working with him. We finished the accounts and walked up the street. He said, "Do you want me to show you the house now?"

We walked into the house. He said, "Do you want to see your room?" and I went upstairs to a lovely room with big open windows. I loved this room.

Journey to Perform Divination by the Moon

The intention is to journey to use the moon to provide us with insight into a question or to give you guidance. You can infer answers from the appearance of the moon, things illuminated by moonbeams, or other communication that you receive. Try to figure out how you are going to use the moon in divination and then do the divination.

Ludivine

I asked where I am going to live in ten years, and the moon was shining around Southeast Asia, like Thailand or Vietnam, somewhere here. After I saw it on a map, and images of like an ancient city, like ruins, like Angkor Wat.

It was like there was war, with refugees, people leaving war.

Pro Tips

The following tips are provided:

1. **Questions.** Divination questions are constructed in a similar way to journey questions, but we can ask closed questions to get "yes" or "no" answers. Questions should relate to practical matters and be specific and unambiguous, which helps get useful answers.

2. **Seriousness.** Divination should be performed for a genuine need, not for amusement. Simple, serious questions are more likely to lead to accurate answers.

3. **Non-reliance.** We should not overly rely on divination for minor decisions or actions.

4. **Use discernment.** When getting answers for others we should use intuition and discern that information we receive is accurate and from an appropriate source.

5. **The future is not fixed.** The future is not pre-determined; a future event divined is a possible one based on your current path; changing this gives a different future.

CHAPTER 2

HEALING

Shamanic healing addresses physical, emotional, mental and spiritual issues, with aims of restoring wholeness, balance, and harmony, and empowerment. Most modalities remove things that do not belong or insert things that do. A key difference between shamanic healing and other healing is that in shamanic healing we heal the dead as well as the living. Shamanic healing is performed by spirits with a practitioner acting as a facilitator. A shamanic healer does not use their personal power in healing but mediates the application of spiritual power.

SHAMANIC HEALING TECHNIQUES

The main shamanic healing techniques can be classified as follows:

1. **Removal modalities:** clearing, extraction, curse removal, depossession.

2. **Insertion modalities:** blessing, shadow work, soul retrieval, destiny retrieval.

3. **Other modalities:** ancestral healing, psychopomp, long-distance healing, earth healing.

Clearing removes energy and cleanses people, objects and spaces. Extraction is the removal of energy that can cause illness. Curse removal is the lifting of curses placed on a person, ancestor, place, or object. Depossession is the removal of a possessing spirit.

Blessing provides power to a person, entity, object or place. Shadow work re-integrates parts that a person has repressed. Soul retrieval finds and returns parts of a person's spirit that have become separated through soul loss. Destiny retrieval returns a person's life purpose.

Ancestral healing involves healing ancestors and clearing overshadowing energy from descendants. Psychopomp involves guiding a ghost to where they should have gone to at death. Many of the above techniques can also be performed remotely by a practitioner. We can also extend the above modalities for use in Earth healing and other work.

Often a number of different approaches are used in addition to one or more of the above modalities, such as bodywork and counselling.

The Wounded Healer

The concept of the wounded healer is based on the idea that to be a healer you have to have healed yourself of a particular wound, enabling you to recognize this wound in others, feel compassion for them, and help them to heal themselves.

In shamanic initiation, a person works with spirit to cure their initiatory illness. They then continue to transform issues in themselves, allowing them to help others with these wounds. The implication is you can only help people who have wounds that you have healed in yourself.

Being a wounded healer is about healing wounds and becoming your true self. We need to distinguish between wounded healers, who help another heal themselves, and healers who act from an ego-based view of being a healer, who may not actually be effective in healing.

You must be detached. You do not need to understand completely how healing works, the important thing is that you trigger healing within a person. If you help other people heal themselves, what are you also doing? You are helping to create other potential healers.

Blessings

In a traditional blessing, a person offers support, love, or good luck from their heart to a person or asks that a deity provide this. In a shamanic blessing, a practitioner asks spirit to give spiritual power and support to a person, animal, land, crop, building, object or event.

A shamanic blessing is a form of power retrieval, and a blessing recipient can reconnect to it and be re-empowered. Blessings often use words, a song, or a dance, which are a means to convey power from spirit to the recipient. Word blessings are usually short and easy to remember, which helps a person repeat and reconnect to them.

The following are situations where a blessing may be an appropriate form of healing:

1. At life transitions like births, weddings, or deaths.

2. To allow a dying person to pass peacefully

3. To mark rites of passage.

4. When you want to honor or celebrate locations or events.

5. At the start or end of projects or journeys.

6. When starting a business or some other organization (or to re-empower one).

7. To bring power into sacred space.

8. To bring power into new or renovated buildings, or when moving into a building.

To perform a shamanic blessing, you journey with an intention that you are empowered by spirit with blessing power to be given to a recipient, or that power is placed in a medium or tool used to hold it temporarily. You may also be given words, a song, a dance, or other action. When you return to physical reality, you pass power to the recipient, in a way that spirit has shown you, or that you are guided to, accompanied by words or actions as relevant. You can also merge with a spirit in physical reality and pass a blessing directly to a person or tool.

You can place power in an object or tool using your hands or by blowing power into it as in a power animal retrieval. You then use the object or tool on the recipient to empower them. The blessing can also be put into a symbol which is then placed on a person or tool.

Tools like rattles, drums or bells can provide a blessing to a person or group. Blessing tools is a way of empowering and awakening them and creating a connection between the tool and you. You ask for a blessing for the tool, typically from the tool spirit, and repeat the blessing when you use it. One medium you can use to carry a blessing is water, which can be drunk, sprinkled or washed in. It is also possible to bless larger bodies of water like springs or rivers.

You can also ask for gifts to be blessed. You are not putting an intention into a gift but asking for power that spirit wants to provide. You do not need to know its meaning. You let the gift go and ask it to bless a person it is given to. You retain no connection with the object gifted.

You can perform a blessing as a group by connecting to a helping spirit or using a blessing that was obtained for this purpose and giving the blessing power to the recipient. This process can be combined with an action like sprinkling the recipient with objects like flower petals. Participants figure out how they will do a group blessing and deliver it. They need to decide who or what the recipient of the blessing is, how the blessing will be done, if participants do it together or alone at the same time, and if it is to be delivered in spiritual or physical reality.

You might also want to include a blessing in your ceremony structure. A good place to do this would be just after you have called in the spirits. You might use a blessing of the form: "May this ceremony proceed for the highest good of all concerned harming none."

Pro Tips

The following tips are provided:

1. **The role of healer.** You are not actually healing but facilitating healing performed by spirits. Do not let your ego become too invested in you being a "healer".

2. **Attachment to outcome.** Do not be too attached to the outcome of healing; be open to what may happen. By being detached, we ensure we do not interfere with the healing. For this reason, it is best not to perform healing for family or close friends.

3. **Failure.** If healing "fails," it can be because the healing is deficient, or a person does not want to be healed or blocks healing. Where somebody dies, it may be what was supposed to happen (and "healing" would be helping a person through this transition).

4. **Placebo effect.** Shamanic healing, like all healing, owes some of its effectiveness to psychosomatic and placebo effects that are healing in and of themselves. Just knowing that somebody else cares for you and wants to help you provides a healing benefit.

5. **Pregnancy.** Unless you are sure there are no effects on a mother or fetus, do not heal pregnant women. Note some aromatherapy oils and herbs can induce abortion.

SHADOW WORK

You create shadow parts when you repress traits or behavior that are viewed negatively by yourself or others. This causes unwanted effects and behavior and may lead to loss of positive traits or abilities. Your shadow comprises these repressed shadow parts and is often referred to in negative terms such as your *inner demon*. In shadow work you find, accept, and integrate shadow parts so you become more whole. Reclaiming your shadow is a prerequisite for working with others. You must deal with your own issues before being able to help them.

Shadow Creation

Why do you repress traits or behavior? To fit in with what other people view as acceptable, or that do not fit your own self-image. This reinforces traits and behavior seen as acceptable and allows you to win approval from others. Such repression starts at a young age and is a result or pressure from your family, peers, teachers, authority figures, and society.

However, this also causes you to lose positive aspects of repressed parts and may lead to the loss of traits or abilities. Men often put fear, sensitivity, and creativity in their shadow, and women anger, assertiveness and sexuality in theirs. When you deny parts, you create enemies that may turn on you and express themselves in poor behavior or illness. This is seen, for example, in eruptions of anger, often at an inappropriate time and place.

You project your shadow onto others: projecting negative shadow parts onto those who show traits you dislike, and positive shadow parts onto those you admire. You unjustly blame others because they have the same shadow parts as you, or have unrealistic views of, or idolize, those who express positive traits you have repressed. If a person receives shadow projections, their shadow may react causing conflict.

There are collective shadows. A family shadow is created if a family holds strong views or values, often carried by a black sheep or in family secrets and passed to descendants. Collective shadows are also created by organizations, cultures, nations, and religions. This results in behavior like intolerance, bigotry, persecution, racism, scapegoating, witch-hunting, war, and genocide.

Shadow Work Indications

Shadow effects are often seen in your behavior and attitudes and are indications of negative or positive shadow parts. This includes being strongly repelled by or attracted to traits in others, inappropriate or cruel behavior, experiencing hostility from others, getting excessive negative or positive feedback from others, laughing at others or lacking a sense of humour, or expressing shadow aggression (often seen in crowd behavior). Shadow parts may cause stress and trauma or result in addictive behavior. They may appear in artwork or dreams.

Shadow Work Benefits

Integrating shadow parts stops them sabotaging you, making you more whole and in control of your life. This allows you to be more self-accepting, have more self-worth, feel compassion for others and judge them less, have healthier relationships, and resolve issues with others. It also lets you remove your contribution to collective shadows. Most importantly, you can live more authentically and manifest your life purpose.

Shadow Work Process

You can work with the archetypal shadow, often seen in myth and stories as a dark or negative character, with your own shadow, or with a family shadow. Individually you cannot heal collective shadows, but by integrating your shadow parts you reduce your contribution to collective shadows.

You journey to find shadow parts, get to understand them, convince them to return to physical reality with you, acknowledge and accept them, and integrate them. Shadow parts may be reluctant to work with you initially. Embodying shadow parts can be done by using masks or created artwork, and by using rituals like dance or recital to give the parts expression.

You can identify shadow parts using techniques other than journeying, and then journey to find them and complete the rest of the process as above, by noticing projections you make onto others or by using keywords or questions to identify shadow parts. You can also ask a helping spirit to point out negative and positive shadow parts.

You can use keywords or questions to identify shadow parts that you can identify by their triggering a strong negative or positive reaction in you. The hardest words to own are ones associated with things you blame on others, and where owning a trait would mean giving up such blame, which is resisted by your ego. Speaking the words aloud can help.

A list of "negative" keywords could include the following: Addict, Aggressive, Alcoholic, Angry, Anorexic, Bitch, Bitter, Bossy, Clingy, Cold, Competitive, Controlling, Coward, Crazy, Cruel, Depressed, Destructive, Dirty, Dishonest, Emotional, Evil, Failure, Fat, Frigid, Gambler, Gossip, Greedy, Hard, Hateful, Idiot, Impatient, Impotent, Impulsive, Indecent, Insecure, Intolerant, Jealous, Know it all, Late, Lazy, Liar, Loser, Martyr, Masochist, Materialistic, Mean, Moody, Nasty, Needy, Negative, Nosy, Obsessive, Patronizing, Obstinate, Perfectionist, Pervert, Pessimistic, Petty, Possessive, Prejudiced, Proud, Racist, Rebel, Repulsive, Rude, Ruthless, Sadist, Sarcastic, Scared, Selfish, Shallow, Sick, Sexist, Slut, Snob, Sulky, Suspicious, Thief, Ugly, Unfaithful, Untidy, Useless, Vain, Vengeful, Violent, Vulgar, Weak, Wicked, Wounded.

A list of "positive" keywords could include the following: Affectionate, Affluent, Ambitious, Artistic, Attractive, Authentic, Brave, Broad-minded, Calm, Capable, Charitable, Clever, Compassionate, Competent, Complete, Confident, Creative, Desirable, Eloquent, Energetic, Enthusiastic, Faithful, Frank, Free, Friendly, Fun, Generous, Gentle, Genuine, Gifted, Good-looking, Happy, Healthy, Honest, Honorable, Humble, Imaginative, Impartial, Independent, Inspired, Intelligent, Intuitive, Joyous, Kind, Loving, Loyal, Magical, Merciful, Modest, Motivated, Optimistic, Passionate, Patient, Peaceful, Positive, Powerful, Practical, Pragmatic, Prepared, Proud, Punctual, Pure, Rational, Realistic, Reasonable, Reliable, Resourceful, Secure, Self-reliant, Sensible, Serene, Sincere, Smart, Sober, Sociable, Spiritual, Strong, Successful, Sympathetic, Tactful, Talented, Tenacious, Tidy, Tolerant, Trusting, Understanding, Versatile, Warm, Whole, Worthy.

The following questions can be used to help identify negative shadow parts:

- What do I dislike in other people?
- Who do I hate or judge the most?

- What do I not want others to know about me?

- What am I afraid of finding out about myself?

- What aspects of myself do I need to transform?

The following questions can be used to help identify positive shadow parts:

- What do I admire in other people?

- Who do I like to love the most?

- What would I want others to admire in me?

- What do I most want to feel about myself?

- When I am old what will I regret not having done?

When you suppress a part, you suppress its opposite aspects. Integrating the negative shadow frees the positive. For example, you may not like others controlling you, but this may relate to controlling tendencies or to unexpressed leadership abilities in yourself. If you express true leadership, you will not be as affected by the controlling behavior of others.

Key Ritual

This comprises two rituals. You first journey to find and retrieve a shadow part. You then make a mask or other form of artwork as a temporary repository for the shadow part, and embody and express the part using the artwork, typically through movement or the spoken word, until you are ready to keep the part embodied. You then continue to integrate the part.

Journey to Find and Retrieve a Shadow Part

The intention is to find, befriend, and retrieve a shadow part. You then embody the part in a mask, other object, or artwork and use this to express the part (preferably publicly).

> #### Ann
>
> The part is anger, boiling rage. I wrestled with it. It fought and swore using the worst profanities. It is angry at everything including me. I plead it is part of me, I understand its anger, and I need it for self-development.

After a long debate it simmered and said it would work with me and I returned with it. Making the mask calmed the fury. When I danced, I felt acceptance and freedom and the energy dissipated. It felt okay not to put it back in the mask.

I journeyed to find out how to integrate it and we sat together and talked. It said what is important is how to use its energy. There was a lot of healing.

How to Do the Key Ritual

Have the intention to journey to find a shadow part that you have repressed, work with it, and persuade it to return. The first time you do this work, ask a helping spirit or power animal to take you to a part you can work with. You may find out about integrating the part or take a separate journey for this. Acknowledging a part may be enough to integrate it.

A part may not easily be found and may hide from you. If you find a part, approach it with respect and confidence. It may be reluctant to work with you due to the way you treated it, and often is angry with you and can be difficult or frightening to deal with. Apologize for your previous treatment of it. Encourage it to talk to you, let it know that it is part of you, you love it and want to be in relationship with it, you belong together and that neither of you is whole without the other. Ask it to tell you about itself, what its gifts are, and what it wants to agree to integrate with you. You can also ask it how it would like you to represent it.

Convince it to return with you so you can work with it in physical reality. If it does not agree to return, keep journeying to it until it does. When you persuade it to return with you, embody it as you would a power animal, and return with the part to physical reality.

The part is still an enemy at this point, so place it into an object until you are ready to work with it. You do this by blowing it into the medium that you will use to produce the mask, picture, story, or other representation of it, in the same way that you insert a power animal.

A mask is useful if you want to use dance or some form of acting to express the part, as it can be worn. Masks should have eyeholes, an opening through which you can breathe and speak, and a means of attaching it to your head (like an elastic band). Decorate the object holding the part as guided by it. Put on the mask, or hold an object, and embody the energy as in any merging ritual. Then dance, act, mime, or read a story or poem about the part, or express it in another way, to get to know it. Doing this helps the part accept you.

When you are finished, if you are ready to keep the part embodied take off the mask or put down the object and start the process of integrating the part, using any guidance it provided. If you are not ready to keep it embodied, place it back into the mask or object and return to work with it later. Repeat the process until you are ready to fully embody and integrate it. The mask of other object can then be disposed of, perhaps in a ritual fire or by burying it.

With artwork you can also produce two images, one to express the negative aspect of the part and the other a positive aspect. The negative image is the one where the part is inserted. When a part is embodied, the negative image can be disposed of and the positive one kept.

Other Rituals

Other rituals that you can perform include: journey to meet the shadow, using art to work with shadow parts, journey to work with the family shadow, and journey to work with a collective shadow of humanity.

Journey to Meet the Shadow

The intention is to journey to meet the archetypal shadow to introduce yourself, find out about its nature, how you can work with your own shadow parts, or to get other advice about doing shadow work.

> #### Ann
>
> I asked to be taken to see the master shadow and how I could work with him. I saw a great, tall figure. My power animals appeared. I asked how I could work with him. He was grumpy. I thought, you're miserable. He said, "I want a gift."
>
> I thought, Okay, he wants a gift, and a blue stone appeared in my hands. I said, "Please accept this gift from me."

He said, "Yes, that will be fine, I will give you what you want," but he definitely wanted payment for it.

I was told to go into what looked like a cave, to look for the shadow part and I might have to ask some questions. I am to cup my hands and take the part and put it in my heart, and when I come back, I take a small flat stone from somewhere near running water, it could be a rock pool or by the sea and put the shadow part into that stone, and after I integrate it, I let it go into running water and I wash my hands.

Using Art to Work with Shadow Parts

The intention is to put parts into paper temporarily. When you are ready to work with the part you then put the paper to your heart and let it merge with you. Allow it to say what they want to say. Describe it in words or pictures. Then write something about how you are going to integrate it and work together. If multiple parts are involved, see if there is a synthesis.

Salina

I made more connection. I felt this cultural heritage I have carried like a burden because I wasn't allowed to express myself fully by the community and religion. I couldn't be true to my authentic self. Sometimes I withdrew and became distant and somewhat cold because of that. Recently I thought about this. In Asia I find that I can live the way I want.

Journey to Work with the Family Shadow

The intention is to journey to find out about our family shadow, how it is expressed, and what we can do to embody parts and stop the shadow being passed to future generations.

Salina

I went up to the upper world on my horse and met my grandma. She had white hair and braids. She told me about something I am aware of, communication in my family and how anger is expressed in a straightforward and hurtful way. Things are blurted out without thinking if it will hurt others.

She explained it is not just my family and that many, once things are argued over, go back to normal. She said I had grown estranged and cannot deal with this temper anymore.

She said I must communicate with my family members individually and try to ensure I am neutral and unemotional in the way I express things otherwise the message will not get through and they will not hear what I say.

I asked what I can do to prevent this from being passed on. She said not to worry about that now, there would be other work to do later, and I would go back for this.

Journey to Work with a Collective Shadow of Humanity

You can work with your shadow or a family one, but on your own cannot heal collective shadows. By doing your shadow work you help reduce collective shadows.

Lucie

The shadow was female abuse. It started with baby girls screaming and being killed. There were images of the ancient times in China where they used to bind their feet, all those images. I cut my part of it. The shadow was a big thing with lots of strings attached to people and some scissors came and I was literally detached from it. What was interesting was that second in line ready to be detached was my sister.

I asked what else I can do, and I heard a voice that I was already sponsoring a charity. I have a little girl in Cambodia I am supporting so she can go to school. It is part of removing myself from the shadow by empowering her.

Instead of nurturing the power some men are scared of females and suppress their power rather than use it for better purposes. By doing all these things a lot of the power from women that is being abused generation after generation, like not being able to access information or go where you want, is removed.

Pro Tips

The following tips are provided:

1. **Ongoing shadow work.** Shadow work is incremental and needs to be repeated.

2. **Using affirmations.** To befriend a positive part, we can affirm we have a quality we admire by stating an affirmation like "I am more courageous." To befriend a negative part, you admit we have a trait, become aware of its value, and then affirm this.

3. **Positive shadow parts.** People tend to resist positive shadow aspects more than they hide negative parts, so it is often more difficult to retrieve positive shadow parts.

4. **Dreams.** We can identify shadow parts by seeing the opposite behavior in dreams to waking life. For example, if we are controlling in daily life, we may be submissive in dreams. A personal or collective shadow often appears in dreams as a character.

5. **Other people.** We unconsciously attract people who have the same shadow parts as us. We tend to react more strongly to the shadow in people of the same sex.

EXTRACTION HEALING

Energy can enter a person's energy body and may cause physical, emotional, mental and spiritual issues. Such energy is called a *spiritual intrusion*. This is not the same as possession. This energy is not necessarily negative, but simply does not belong in a person's energy field and may be positive in another context. Extraction healing removes this energy. Extraction healing can be done as a standalone healing modality, or in preparation for some other types of healing, such as soul retrieval.

Causes of Spiritual Intrusions

Intrusions can be caused several ways. Energy may be encountered randomly, picked up from the energy fields of others, or consciously or unconsciously sent to a person or taken from a source. A person may send energy to someone else when emotions like anger are expressed. Energy may be received as a result of trauma, injury, illness, or a loss of personal power. Energy may also be transferred from a parasite or received as the result of an organ transplant.

Extraction Healing Indications

Spiritual intrusion indications include localized pain or discomfort, chronic stress or anxiety with no obvious cause, lethargy, reliving traumatic or upsetting events, having negative self-feelings, a history of abusive relationships, temperature increase (due to the energy) or the presence of blocks in your energy body.

Extraction Healing Benefits

Benefits of extraction healing include the removal or chronic physical pain or illness, feeling physically stronger, feeling mentally and emotionally balanced, feeling more light-hearted, and clearing your energy body of stagnant energy.

Extraction Healing Process

In extraction healing, you journey to a helping spirit and ask them to perform extraction healing for you. You can also perform extraction healing for another person in physical reality. This requires that you can merge with a helping spirit. Some form of empowerment is then done for yourself or the other person, to fill holes in your or their energy field where intruding energy has been removed. Long-term avoidance of intrusions is facilitated by a person becoming more empowered, which makes it much harder for intrusions to enter them.

If you have journeyed to ask for extraction healing for yourself, one of your helping spirits will perform his ritual for you and can then also empower you. If you are performing extraction healing for another person, merge with a power animal or other helping spirit, scan the person's body to detect intrusions, remove them as you are guided, and release the intruding energy. You then empower the person. This is a non-invasive process where you use your hands or an object to remove intrusions.

In traditional cultures, energy could also be sucked out of a person, the practitioner in such traditions described with a term such as a *sucking doctor*. This involves some danger to the practitioner who could take the energy into their own bodies and be affected by it. To prevent this, intrusion energy would typically be captured in material such as tobacco, placed in the practitioner's mouth, which would be spat out removing intrusion energy. It is recommended that this form of extraction healing is not used due to the potential danger to the practitioner.

Key Ritual: Journey to Ask for Extraction Healing for Yourself

The intention is to journey to ask a spirit to perform extraction healing on you.

Maya

I went to the lower world and met my horse spirit animal. I get out of the water and there is a sand dune where the Horse laid me out. He did the healing by opening me up with his hoof. Inside were these little black bubbles. He took out all the bubbles. Then he showed me that you can suck them and expel them. He was breathing out through his nostrils some really clean white energy, a cleansing energy.

He then wanted me to see that it could be done without the hoof method. He used the hoof to seal my body and then we were both looking at my body. He showed me some more bubbles by my left shoulder and how he could just pluck it out without breaking the skin. There was also something by the throat that was more slimy energy. He sent the black bubbles and the slimy stuff away. He said the energy will change. I didn't ask about the process.

Then he put in quartz crystals and selenite, the one that is self-cleansing. I asked why but he didn't really respond. I think it was cleansing and would keep regenerating in a healthy way. Also, the quartz crystal was meant to magnify the selenite, that is what I understood.

How to Do the Key Ritual

Have the intention to journey to a helping spirit or a power animal. Ask the spirit if they can perform extraction healing for you or if they can take you to meet another spirit who will perform this healing if they are not going to do it themselves. Usually, the helping spirit will do the extraction healing for you.

Ask the helping spirit if there is anything that you need to do first. If not, then follow any instructions that they spirit gives you and be open to receive the healing.

Allow the spirit to perform the extraction healing. This should not result in discomfort, no matter how dramatic the extract healing process may be. For example, the spirit may cut your body in order to retrieve energy, and energy extracted may take a number of forms. This could be dark colored smoke, an object such as a rock, or structures like cords.

The helping spirit or power animal may insert something into your body after they have performed the extraction healing. This could be power or a power object such as a crystal. The helping spirit may perform empowerment in another way, such as passing energy into your body with their hands, singing it into you, or performing an action such as a dance that empowers you.

When the healing is complete, thank the helping spirit, make them an offering or ask if there is anything else that they would like you to do for them, and then return to physical reality.

Other Rituals

Other rituals that you can perform include: journey to meet a helping spirit for extraction healing, journey to learn an empowerment technique, and journey to perform extraction healing for another person.

Journey to Meet a Helping Spirit for Extraction Healing

The intention is to journey to meet a spirit to get guidance on how to prepare for or do extraction. This could be an existing power animal or helping spirit, or a new spirit you only work with for this modality. If you meet a spirit, introduce yourself, and ask for any guidance they have for you.

Sue

> I went to a clearing in the forest. My spirit animals came out, then a tree walked out. We greeted each other. I explained I was looking to find out how to do extraction healing and wanted to know who to work with, and the tree stepped forward.
>
> I felt the tree and could feel energy coming up through my feet and my body felt dense. As I merged more, I felt really tall. I gradually worked my way up through the tree and ended up at the top.
>
> My third eye was tingling, and I felt surges of energy flowing through, coming through the roots and coming up and spreading across, flowing out everywhere. It suggested using a branch to create a vortex to use in the actual extraction healing.

Journey to Learn an Empowerment Technique

The intention is to journey to a helping spirit to fins out how to perform empowerment for a person after you have completed an extraction healing for them.

Sue

> I asked what I could do while merged to empower another person and it just said allow the energy to flow, and it will calm and relax and go where it needs to go. When I call it here, I call it up through my feet and legs from the earth. The energy is gentle, ancient, calming.

Journey to Perform Extraction Healing for Another Person

The intention is to scan a person's energy fields to diagnose the presence of spiritual intrusions. These are removed and an empowerment performed for the person, in this example using elemental and lunar energy to empower and balance elemental energies.

Partially merge with a helping spirit and perform diagnosis by passing your hands or a tool such as a feather over a person's body to sense intrusions. Intrusions may be detected by a change in movement of your hand or the tool, or a temperature difference. You can also use vision to detect intrusions, which may appear as dark shapes, sharp objects, or insects.

Having established that intrusions are present, fully merge with a helping spirit to perform the healing. Remove intrusions from a person's energy field as guided. This can be with the hands or a power object. We can also use the spirit's energetic anatomy. For instance, if merged with a bird spirit, you can remove intrusions with the spirit's wingtips.

Place removed spiritual intrusion energy in water or salt, send it into fire to transform it, or intend to send it directly to the earth or sun to be transformed and made available for re-use, or as you are otherwise guided. Extraction is complete when you detect no intrusions by repeating the diagnosis or the spirit informs you it is complete. Rattle over the person with an intention to clear any residual intrusion energy.

After extraction healing, fill any holes in their energy body by power animal retrieval, giving them empowered water to drink, or a healing technique like passing power from spirit via hands on healing. Disengage from spirit at the end of the extraction healing session.

Mark

> I tell the client that I will first find any issues in her energy fields and will then resolve them. I tell her that I will later place my hands on the top of her shoulders to do some hands-on healing and ask if this is okay. She confirms it is.
>
> I call eagle to me and merge lightly with it, feeling the presence of the spirit and sensing the outlines of its form covering my body, eagle's wings extending beyond my hands and arms. I place my left hand over the client's head perpendicular to the floor with the fingers pointing away from me. The hand starts to shake lightly, and I move it slowly down the client's head to sense intrusions.
>
> Reaching the throat area, the hand starts to shake more vigorously, indicating an intrusion. Sometimes the hand also turns so that it is now parallel to the floor and the action more resembles the hand flapping toward the intrusion. "There is something blocking or restricting your

throat chakra. This usually indicates some form of communication issue." The client confirms that she sometimes has trouble saying what she feels.

My hand moves down the client's arms and the motion changes back to the initial movement. There are no issues there and I then move down her center line. The heart is okay, but the shaking becomes more vigorous again in the area of the solar plexus, which is where the third chakra is located. "There is also an issue with the third chakra. This is to do with your personal power. You may not be fully expressing your power, acting as a powerful woman in the world." The client nods her head.

Moving my hand over her legs I find what I expect to see, more widespread random movements indicating a general area of stuck or clogged energy. "You also seem to have some stagnant energy in your lower body which probably means that you might have trouble grounding yourself fully."

I merge fully with eagle. I feel its presence much more strongly. I point my two hands toward the client's throat area with the fingers together and above her throat, knowing that the spirit's wing tips are within her energy body. I help eagle to remove the intrusion by making a scooping motion with my hands and then throwing this energy toward the earth (with the intention that it is re-used after being transformed). After I have done this a couple of times I re-scan her throat with my hand to confirm that the intrusion has been removed. The hand movement is now normal.

I repeat this process for the other two areas, the solar plexus area needing more work. For the legs I often use a clawing motion with the hands above the legs to do the extraction.

Having completed the first part, I now sit behind the client's head and, still merged with eagle, call the power of the four elements to me, visualizing them in their powerful forms as I do: air as a tornado, fire as the heart of a star, water as a tidal wave, and earth as an earthquake.

As the client is female, I also reach a hand up and draw down power from the moon. This lunar energy is silver, feminine and immensely powerful. It is beautiful energy. I tell the client to be open to receive energy I am going to pass to her and place my hands on her shoulders and intend strongly to pass the power to her so that it fills any holes in her energy fields and helps to balance elemental energies within her.

This process takes a minute or so. I ask the client how the energy makes her feel. She tells me it makes her feel peaceful and calm. I am intending a feeling of tranquillity in addition to empowerment. The healing is complete.

Pro Tips

The following tips are provided:

1. **Talking about intrusions.** Often a person is interested in what was seen or removed. It is best to discourage discussion as it can traumatise them if negative images are described or empower intrusions through fear or anger. Focus on positive aspects of the healing, like what did not belong has been removed, which facilitates healing.

2. **Intrusion elusiveness.** Intrusions may move and try to hide from a practitioner.

3. **Intrusions or possession?** Intrusions and spirit possession cause similar symptoms and it can be difficult to tell the difference. The localised nature of intrusions is one way to differentiate them from possession. You can also confirm the nature of the illness and required treatment via divination or communication with a helping spirit.

4. **Disposing of intrusion energy.** Take care when discarding of extracted intrusion energy. It should not be left somewhere where it may affect others.

5. **Symbology.** If something is seen or sensed during extraction healing, this is a symbol that can provide information about its nature or the cause of the spiritual intrusion.

SOUL RETRIEVAL

Parts of a person's soul may leave for a variety of reasons, including a person experiencing trauma or a part being taken. These parts are separate from the person and can be located anywhere in spiritual reality. Such soul loss, or soul theft, causes a number of issues including a loss of personal power, and a person not being able to live their life purpose authentically due to lacking parts of themselves, traits associated with those parts, or personal power.

In soul retrieval a person journeys to spiritual reality to ask for soul retrieval for themselves or to find one or more soul parts for another person. In the case of the latter, the person persuades parts to return with them and inserts them into a person's energy body. The person then must integrate these parts of themselves to complete the healing.

Causes of Soul Loss

Why do soul parts leave? A soul part may leave if it does not feel safe, does not want to stay, or is trying to escape pain. Soul loss can occur at any time but is especially associated with childhood, puberty, or teenage years. For instance, a part may leave at puberty due to a fear of sexual activity or sexual abuse and to avoid experiencing this.

The main causes of soul loss are suffering a traumatic experience such as an accident or some form of abuse, relationship problems, being dominated by a person or group, issues such as fear or grief, being unable to move past an event, or addictions or compulsive behavior. A soul part may also go with a removed body part, or due to the effects of anaesthetic.

A person may give parts of themselves to others, often to appease another or to try to maintain a relationship. If this happens then, when the other person leaves or dies, their soul parts can leave with the other person.

Soul theft can be by people or spirits and is often done out of ignorance. Soul theft is usually done to try to get the power of a person or power over them, or to try to keep a connection to another dead or live person. We should be compassionate to a soul thief as they are also often victims. Children are especially susceptible to soul theft and may become introverted and self-protective if this occurs.

If a soul part if surrendered or soul theft occurs a person is weaker, and this may create a pattern of soul theft or giving up soul parts as a means of dealing with issues like abuse. This is bad for both parties. The person who has lost the soul part is not whole; the person who has their soul part has energy that does not belong to them that they cannot necessarily use and that may affect them in some way.

Soul Loss Indications

Soul loss indications include feeling incomplete or outside your body, being unable to move past an issue, having emotions like anger or fear you cannot explain, having chronic issues like depression (especially in childhood), having phobias and anxieties, having memory gaps (due to a memory being with a part), and continuing unhealthy or addictive behavior or thoughts.

If soul loss has occurred, people may become introverted and self-protective. Another indicator is someone being strongly attracted to the idea of soul retrieval. You may also indirectly detect soul loss in a person's language, especially the use of phrases such as "They took a piece of me when they left" or "I have not felt the same since [some past event]."

Soul Retrieval Benefits

The initial effects of soul retrieval may include disorientation, emotions like sadness or anger, or the return of memories of past events. These typically fade after a few days. Long-term effects and benefits include feeling more present and complete, having more energy, being able to move past issues and make changes such as ending abusive relationships or giving up addictive or compulsive behavior, losing feelings or emotions that you struggled with, being more joyful, the disappearance of phobias, and the return of trait or abilities and memories.

Soul Retrieval Process

In soul retrieval, you journey to a helping spirit and ask them to perform soul retrieval for yourself, or journey to perform soul retrieval for another person. One or more soul parts are typically found and retrieved.

If you have journeyed to ask for soul retrieval for yourself, one or more soul parts are retrieved by a helping spirit and inserted into you directly in the journey. You then return to physical reality with the parts. The spirit may give you advice about integrating the parts.

If you are journeying to perform soul retrieval for another person, you search for one or more soul parts, convince them to come back with you, place them in your heart chakra or a shamanic tool, and then return to physical reality with the parts and blow them into the heart and crown chakras of the person who is to receive them. You may again get advice soul part integration. The person who has received the soul part(s) then begins to integrate them by welcoming them and being open to working with them as they are guided.

In soul retrieval, you or a spirit are trying to convince parts to return to a person. It therefore helps to perform preparatory work aimed at making the person who will receive the part(s) as pure as possible. This can be done by clearing or ritual bathing by a person prior to having soul retrieval. It may also be helpful to perform healing work such as extraction healing prior to soul retrieval, to remove energy that is not part of a person's natural energy body.

Key Ritual: Journey to Ask for a Soul Retrieval for Yourself

The intention is to journey to ask one of your helping spirits to do a soul retrieval for you.

Maya

> I went to my sacred space and I met my horse. He said he
> would help me, and we flew to a cave. It was not a place
> I had been to before; it was dark and gray, and I thought
> "What is this?"

> My bear power animal came, and he went and got the
> piece of my soul. It all happened very quickly. It was just
> so beautiful, he held it in his claws in a ball. He brought

it to me, and I was just saying you know like, "You're welcome, I'm sorry, I love you." It came into me and then the bear put his hand up and sealed it in.

I went through all these crazy emotions when it first came in. I was really upset. Bear told me something had happened where I had a big fall. That is all he would tell me. I asked if I could do anything for him or if he could do some healing. He cut me open and took something out.

My horse came and we flew back to the sacred space. Then the drumming sounded to return, and I came back.

How to Do the Key Ritual

Have the intention to journey to a helping spirit or a power animal. Ask the spirit if they can perform soul retrieval for you, or if they can take you to meet another spirit who will perform the soul retrieval if they are not going to do it themselves. Usually, the helping spirit will do the soul retrieval for you.

Ask the helping spirit if there is anything that you need to do first. If there is, you or the helping spirit may take some action. If not, then follow any other instructions that the spirit gives you and be open to receive the healing.

Allow the helping spirit to perform the soul retrieval. They may go to find the soul part, in which case wait for them to return with it. It may also be possible that they call a soul part to them, or they may even have the part with them when you journey to meet them.

The soul part may appear as a ball or a bright energetic object or may look like a smaller and younger version of you. The spirit will then insert the soul part into you by placing it into your heart chakra or blowing it in to your heart. Alternatively, the soul part may fly into your body of its own accord in some manner.

The helping spirit may insert something else into your body after they have performed the soul retrieval. This could be a power animal that comes with the soul part or a power object of some kind.

When the healing is complete, thank the helping spirit, make them an offering, or ask if there is anything else that they would like you to do for them, and then return to physical reality.

Other Rituals

Other rituals that you can perform include: journey to meet a helping spirit for soul retrieval, journey to perform soul retrieval for another person, ritual to release soul parts of other people, and journey to get a ritual to call your soul parts home.

Journey to Meet a Helping Spirit for Soul Retrieval

The intention is to journey to meet a spirit to get guidance on how to prepare for or do soul retrieval. This could be an existing power animal or helping spirit, or a new spirit you only work with for this modality. If you meet a spirit, introduce yourself, and ask for any guidance they have for you.

> #### Sophia
>
> I journeyed and asked the teaching spirit I was working with, but the spirit said, "Come back later, you need to understand a bit more before I can teach you on this topic." It was the spirit of the snake I should work with initially. It will accompany me on the process. I got some guidance that I should feel things relevant to the soul part. I asked if I needed to use tools or if anything else was relevant, but I didn't get anything else.

Journey to Perform a Soul Retrieval for Another Person

The intention is to perform soul retrieval for another person by journeying to find soul parts that belong to them, convincing the soul parts to return with you, and then returning with the soul parts to physical reality and inserting them into the person's body.

The first thing is to confirm that soul retrieval is appropriate for a person who asks for it, based on prior work that they have done and your perception of their ability to integrate parts. If a person has done no work previously with you and has not received any form of shamanic healing previously, they are probably not ready to receive soul retrieval.

Somebody that you have not worked with but who has received shamanic healing from other practitioners may well be able to receive soul retrieval. Someone that you have worked with before you will know more about and will be able to decide or be guided as to their preparedness for soul retrieval. You can use divination to confirm soul retrieval is appropriate.

If a person is not ready to receive soul retrieval then explain this to them, together with an indication of work that they need to do to allow soul retrieval to be performed in the future. This might involve preparatory work such as extraction healing or allowing time for this to be integrated by the person. You may also perform empowerment rituals described earlier.

If a person is ready to receive soul retrieval, confirm they understand that this healing can result in significant change. A practitioner may also suggest soul retrieval healing to an existing client of theirs that they feel or are guided is ready to receive it.

Send the person some overview information, a week or so ahead of the time that the soul retrieval healing is booked, about soul retrieval, possible results, and any preparation they need to do prior to the healing. On the day of the healing explain the soul retrieval process to them again and answer any questions that they have. Explain that soul parts retrieved will be blown into their body heart and crown chakras when you have finished the soul retrieval journey. Confirm they are okay with the physical contact involved in the healing.

The person can undertake two optional preparatory rituals to release other people's parts they are holding and to call their soul parts home (see below for a description of these journeys). Again, you can use a divination ritual to see if these are appropriate.

Begin the healing itself by clearing the person to help make them as pure as possible to receive any soul parts that you can retrieve for them. Have the person lie on a treatment table or on a yoga mat on the floor and provide them with a pillow and blanket if they want these. Lie or sit next to the person and tell them to be open to receiving soul parts of theirs that agree to return. For the avoidance of doubt, the person who will receive soul parts does not journey!

In the literature, reference is sometimes made to maintaining body contact with the person during a soul retrieval. This may break your concentration, so this is up to you. I sit next to the person and will sometimes hold their hand or rest my hand on their arm.

Journey with the intention to find any soul parts willing to return. Sometimes you must go to difficult places to find soul parts, and may be subjected to a test, trial, or ordeal to obtain a part. This may be to prove you are sincere, are willing to face your fears to help a person or have enough power to look after the part.

You should be prepared, within reason, to go wherever you need to and to do whatever is necessary to retrieve parts. Some parts are easily found while others may be difficult to get. If you cannot find or see a part, you can also try to call it and it may come to us. If needed, you can ask a helping spirit to assist.

When a part is found, persuade it to return to the person by talking to it. Introduce yourself, explain that you are there to help, find out why it left, and convince it that the situation that caused it to leave no longer applies and it is safe for it to return. Sometimes you are provided with details about why a part left, but only need to know relevant details and may not know the full story.

Explain that the person wants the part to return and this is in both their interest as neither is complete otherwise. Parts usually agree to return, although this may take a while with angry or stubborn parts. If a part does not agree to return you can always try to retrieve it another time, and in the meantime find another part.

Something may be guarding and protecting the part, like a power animal, which may want to return with the part. Sometimes a talisman or power object may be offered by spirit to be taken back with the part.

Retrieving a stolen part may or may not be possible. A soul thief may (incorrectly) feel they need a part and is often unwilling to give it up. Engage in dialogue with the thief and convince them to release it, perhaps offering a gift or bribe. You still need to engage the part in dialogue as above to convince it to return voluntarily. You may be able to help the soul thief, who may also have suffered soul loss (doing a retrieval for them is one way of getting the person's part).

If a part agrees to return, put it in your heart chakra or a tool like a crystal. Then try to find other parts. A retrieved part may recommend other parts, help find them, convince them to return, or carry parts back to physical reality. In one session, retrieve three parts at most, as a person would have trouble integrating more parts. Parts can suggest a ritual to welcome them back when retrieved, or a person can determine this during integration of a part.

Return to physical reality with the soul part(s), blow them into the person's heart and crown chakras (through the object if one was used), and rattle around these chakras to seal the parts in the person's body. Welcome the soul parts back verbally.

Then discuss the retrieval with the person and recount events that occurred and information you received about why the part(s) left if this is useful to the person. You may also have received guidance to relay to the person. Remind them that you do not know if the information received is literal or metaphorical, so they must decide what is relevant for them.

You should consider what information is appropriate to share with the person. They may not be aware of the circumstances that led a part to leave, especially if these are traumatic. Do not share information if you suspect it may traumatize them. If you retrieve a part held by a living person, it is best not to mention this as it can create guilt in the person who held the part if they find out about this subsequently.

In general, we focus on healing rather than the trauma associated with soul loss, and that what is being returned is a pure part, not trauma associated with loss. Discourage discourse on events that led to soul loss; instead focus on positives. Stress that the soul part is back, they are more complete, and have more power. The person may not fully understand how or why a part left and may not relate to information provided. They may also not remember an event immediately. Sometimes symbols or events that do not make sense to the practitioner have deep meaning for the person receiving the healing.

Allow the person to ask questions and explain next steps. The person should engage with the returned part(s) via journey, dream work, or meditation, and enter into dialogue with them to welcome them and thank them for returning, to ask what needs to be done for them to stay, to find out how to honor them, and to find out how to integrate them (perhaps with a ritual suggested by the part). People can honor soul parts by placing representations of them on an altar. Soul loss involves power loss, so it may be appropriate to do an empowerment or power animal retrieval if this was not done as part of the soul retrieval. Modalities such as bodywork or counseling may also be considered in conjunction with soul retrieval.

Confirm you are available to assist the person with any issues and make sure that somebody is available to help them with any issues that may arise as a result of the soul retrieval.

Lilian

> I went to the upper world with hawk and I felt a lot of fire energy. I came to a place where there was a wall of fire and it was saying I had to go through this wall to get to this part that was on the other side.
>
> So, I went through, and a little girl was in a garden, but all around the garden were the flames. I said, "Are you a piece of [the person's] soul?" She said yes, but she was sullen and petulant, and didn't really want to talk. She was upset and angry.
>
> So, I made some comment like my name is Lilian and [the person] really wants you to come back to be with her and be a part of her. I said, "How old are you?" and she said three or three and a half. She said something had happened, she fell into some kind of water and I had an image of her being underwater and she was afraid and angry and felt [the person] wasn't looking after her, and I guess she felt threatened, so she left.
>
> So, we spoke for a bit and I convinced her to come along. When she was about to come, she said had a little pet in the place. In this garden they had a pond; her pet was a little turtle. So, I said, "Okay, let me check with my spirits if this is also something I should be bringing back." The spirit guide said yes, it was a companion for this piece in this place and they could both come back together, so I brought them both back.

Ritual to Release Soul Parts of Other People

You may have taken parts of others (or others may have given parts to you). You may be holding parts of people who are alive or dead. Journey to or communicate with a spirit helper to see if you are holding parts of other people, how this arose, and ask for a short ritual to release parts belonging to others. Examples of rituals that can be used:

1. **Candle.** Light a candle, look at the flame and focus on the intention to release parts. When ready blow the flame out visualizing parts being taken on the smoke to spirit.

2. **Breath.** Focus on the intention to release parts as you inhale and then exhale and visualize the parts being released with your breath.

3. **Fire.** Use a small fire to burn material representing soul parts, like pieces of sage, intended that parts are taken on the smoke from the fire to spirit.

4. **Nature.** Go into nature and find an object like a stick that you break to signify releasing any hold you have on soul parts belonging to others.

Often just acknowledging you have someone's part is enough to release it. When you perform a ritual to release parts do not send them back to the people they belong to, as you do not have permission to do this. Intend to release them so they are available to return to a person. They may return of their own accord or be found if soul retrieval is done for that person.

If you know whose soul parts you have been holding, after you release them you may notice positive changes in your relationship with the person or in their life. This type of ritual can be repeated at intervals to ensure that you release parts you may have taken or been given.

Journey to Get a Ritual to Call Your Soul Parts Home

The intention is to journey to ask for a ritual you can use to call any of your own soul parts that are ready to return to you. The ritual can be performed in physical reality after a journey or in spiritual reality during a journey. This may work for parts easily persuaded to return.

> *Salina*
>
> I wrote down my intention in an old leather book and when I had finished, I had to let the sheet of paper go on the wind. A Native American said the eagle will bring them back to me. The eagle brought a box. When he opened it, a ball of energy came back into me.

Pro Tips

The following tips are provided:

1. **Family and friends.** It is inappropriate to perform soul retrieval on family and friends. You are too familiar with their life history, which may influence you, and you are too invested in the outcome and lack the impartiality required for effective healing.

2. **Children.** You can do soul retrievals on children but need permission of both parents. We should explain things using terms a child understands and is comfortable with.

3. **The dead.** A soul part may be held by a dead person (or a person may be holding a part of a dead person). Soul parts with or of dead people are not unclean but pure.

4. **Gifting a tool.** If a crystal or other tool was used this may also be given as a gift to the person as a memento and reminder of the soul retrieval.

5. **Long-term changes.** Spiritual work often produces long-term changes in people and their relationships, careers and worldview. This is especially so with soul retrieval.

DESTINY RETRIEVAL

Before you are born, you agree to a life purpose with helping spirits. As you are born, you forget this purpose. Destiny retrieval lets you remember your life purpose, helping you to do what you came here to do. There are several ways in which you may retrieve aspects of your own destiny by journeying to a specific location or object, or to one or more destiny related spirits. A practitioner may also journey to retrieve knowledge of another person's destiny.

Why You Forget Your Destiny

Why do you forget your destiny at the point that you are born? In order to grow and develop, you would want to be able to experience and learn new things, in lifetimes where you perhaps have a different gender, race, belief system or personality, or live in a different time period. You might want to have different life experiences, some of which may be challenging.

None of this would be possible if you could recall your life purpose, or past life experiences. If you do not recall these, you can learn life lessons and experience spiritual growth without being affected by past lives. You may also be in relationship with souls that you incarnate with, and memory of past life events might preclude you being able to be in such relationships with those that have harmed you or you have harmed. You should experience and learn new things.

Destiny Retrieval Indications
There are several indications that you are not living your life purpose. This includes feeling that your life lacks meaning, that you are resigned to your fate, that you are not living the life you should be, if you suffer from disillusionment and apathy, or if you are living a life characterized by materialist, narcissistic, and self-serving attitudes and behavior. Addictions, suicidal tendencies, and immune system diseases may also be indicators. If you make changes that are more in alignment with your destiny, positive changes occur and you are aligned with your purpose, even if you still may not know exactly what this is.

Destiny Retrieval Benefits
Destiny retrieval can positively impact your current life, providing a feeling of your life having purpose and meaning and being worth living, and that you are doing what you are supposed to. Old behavior patterns and negative feelings or limiting beliefs can be removed. You may also be able to have a more spiritual, creative, or service-focused life. You will have a more positive view of aging and death if your life has purpose and you feel fulfilment with your destiny.

Destiny Retrieval Process
In destiny retrieval, you journey to a helping spirit and ask them to perform destiny retrieval for yourself, or journey to perform destiny retrieval for another person. The intention is that the highest possible destiny in this incarnation is found and retrieved.

If you have journeyed to ask for destiny retrieval for yourself, the destiny is retrieved by a helping spirit and inserted into you directly in the journey. You then return to physical reality with the destiny.

If you are journeying to perform destiny retrieval for another person, you search for a destiny, convince it to come back with you, place it in your heart chakra or a shamanic tool, and then return to physical reality with the destiny and blow it into the heart and crown chakras of the person who is to receive it. The person who has received the destiny then begins to integrate it, typically being advised by a helping spirit or by a practitioner what is needed for this.

You can journey to a specialist spirit to help with decisions at a key turning point, or to a symbolic object associated with destiny, such as a book or a star.

Spirits associated with destiny include triple goddesses, seen across cultures. They include the Greek Moirai (Fates), the Roman Parcae, the Norse Norns, and the Wyrd Sisters. These spirits are associated with spinning or weaving symbols like wool, thread, spindles, spinning wheels, the moon (symbolic of a spinning wheel), and the world tree.

A book of destiny has a destiny within it. Sometimes this can be changed, including a person's lifespan. A repository may also be tablets or a tapestry. Books are often multi-dimensional and contain portals you can enter. A star of destiny is a spirit that controls destiny. There is a generic star that controls multiple destinies. Each person also has an individual star.

Another destiny symbol is a crossroads. There is often a choice of three or four ways, leading you toward or away from your destiny. You can work at a crossroads or journey to spirits associated with crossroads to help with choices. Crossroad spirits are often tricksters. Both mandalas and medicine wheels are associated with crossroads.

It may be helpful to perform other healing work prior to destiny retrieval. This could include extraction healing, which helps to remove things from your past and present and allow you to receive a new energetic structure that allows you to embrace your destiny. It also helps to remove clutter from your life, attachments to people or things that no longer serve you, resolve issues with others, and discover and remove blocks such as limiting beliefs.

Key Ritual: Journey to Retrieve a Destiny for Yourself

The intention is to journey to ask one of your helping spirits to retrieve a destiny for you or to help you find your destiny.

Sophia

> The spirit changed to three threads which I held on to and it took me to where I needed to go and went into visions of what my destiny was. My destiny was to do with being connected with a charity that restores balance between the relationship between people and nature and being very involved in this charity. I think I was running the charity. It was in Australia. I could see myself doing things with it. I asked questions about how I get there but that wasn't answered in the journey.

How to Do the Key Ritual

Have the intention to journey to a helping spirit or a power animal. Ask the spirit if they can perform destiny retrieval for you or if they can take you to meet another spirit who will perform this healing if they are not going to do it themselves. Usually, the helping spirit will do the destiny retrieval for you. You may also be taken by the spirit to help find your destiny which you then retrieve yourself.

Ask the helping spirit if there is anything that you need to do first. If not, then follow any instructions that they spirit gives you and be open to receive the healing. Allow the helping spirit to perform the destiny retrieval. They may go to find the destiny in which case wait for them to return with it. It may also be possible that they call a destiny to them, or they may even have the destiny with them when you journey to meet them. The destiny may appear as a symbol or object. The spirit will then insert the destiny into you by placing it into your heart chakra or blowing it in to your heart. Alternatively, the destiny may fly into your body of its own accord in some manner.

The helping spirit may insert something else into your body after they have performed the destiny retrieval. This could be a power animal that comes with the destiny or a power object of some kind.

When the healing is complete, thank the helping spirit, make them an offering, or ask if there is anything else that they would like you to do for them, and then return to physical reality.

You could also look for your own destiny by searching along individual timelines (or in the web of collective destinies) to find possible destinies. You are usually guided to a relevant one (often seen as a luminous thread), the highest potential destiny for you in this lifetime.

Other Rituals

Other rituals that you can perform include: journey to meet a helping spirit for destiny retrieval, journey to retrieve a destiny for another person, journey to the Wyrd Sisters, journey to your book of destiny, journey to your star of destiny, journey to the crossroads, and journey to find out about the collective destiny of humans.

Journey to Meet a Helping Spirit for Destiny Retrieval

The intention is to journey to meet a spirit to get guidance on how to prepare for or do destiny retrieval. This could be an existing power animal or helping spirit, or a new spirit you only work with for this modality. If you meet a spirit, introduce yourself, and ask for any guidance they have for you. Thank any spirit that helped you and return.

> *Lucie*
>
> It was like a Chinese Emperor, it looked like that, very grand, all in gold and red, very beautiful clothes. He wanted me to call him Grandpa. He gave me a cross with arms the same length. At the center there was a lotus flower. He told me it would help me in retrieving my destiny. I would have to follow the lotus flower. I can also use that flower to help me fetch other people's destinies as well.

Journey to Retrieve a Destiny for Another Person

The intention is to journey to search for a destiny of another person. The destiny once found is then brought back to physical reality and blown into the person's heart and crown chakras in the same way that a soul part is returned in soul retrieval.

When retrieving a destiny for a person, you can ask a destiny helping spirit to help or search along individual timelines (or in the web of collective destinies) to find possible destinies. You are usually guided to a relevant one (often seen as a luminous thread), the highest potential destiny for the individual in this lifetime.

It is possible that you may be guided to perform soul retrieval during a destiny retrieval, or to perform destiny retrieval during a soul retrieval.

Mark

I called for the thread and I could see it. It was gold and I followed it and it started twisting and got faster like a roller coaster. Then it started growing leaves and finally after quite a while it came up into the head of a lotus. The destiny was in the middle like a little diamond or star. I thought it was really beautiful.

I took the destiny. I knew what it was going to be about. They said it is to do with compassion. I said, "I know it is about power." That is the meaning of compassion. Her destiny is to be a woman of power and that is what has been enabled. This piece is the power. She has the power and compassion.

Journey to the Wyrd Sisters

The Anglo-Saxon Wyrd Sisters weave a cloth for each person corresponding to their energy. This is left in a cave in spiritual reality that each person has to find. The more a person's life pattern matches the cloth's, the more harmonious it is. In this journey you intend to meet the Wyrd Sisters and/or find your cloth to understand our destiny.

Sue

I was going down through a tunnel like the *Indiana Jones* mine train, going down through the earth. I was following a red light and as I got to where I was going to be there were wispy figures flying around the cart. I ended up in a cave and the three of them were sitting around a fire. They were wearing black cloaks with hoods. The younger one was doing the talking.

The message I got was their job is more to weave the destinies and they are impartial observers, they are not going to help, just to set it up and then it was up to me to find my way through it. I asked how I was going to find my destiny and they said follow the light.

They said people plan their destinies beforehand and the closer to the path they are the more right it feels. I said you do not always get the best experiences on your path and they said that doesn't matter you always get the feeling that this is the right way to go than any other way and still feel energised.

Journey to Your Book of Destiny

Here we journey to our individual Book of Destiny to read about our destiny. In more advanced work we can also look at making changes to this destiny if relevant and agreed by our helping spirits. This journey can also be done by a practitioner on behalf of a person.

James

I saw a book which was big. I had a look at it, and someone came and started ripping out pages and it got smaller; but as it got smaller it got more beautiful and was shining and more precise. There was a guy like Merlin who went up to a library and put my book in a shelf next to my family's books. My kids have to go through their own journey, but my book is influencing them.

Journey to Your Star of Destiny

Here we journey to the Star of Destiny (the generic star of a person's individual star). This journey can also be done by a practitioner on behalf of a person.

Ann

I just saw this huge star and I merged with it. Then I just sat inside it for the whole of the time and it was very, very fabulous. I didn't ask anything, I just sat there. I was thinking I should ask questions and then thought no, I am just going to sit here. I sat there and it was glorious.

Journey to the Crossroads

The intention is to journey to a crossroads to ask to understand why we may be stuck, obtain advice on the choices before us, and assist us with a decision or life transition. The crossroads may offer a choice of ways forward, or a decision to stay where we are, go back, or go forward. Spirits traditionally associated with crossroads include Hermes (four-way crossroads) and Hecate (three-way crossroads).

> ### Sue
>
> It was night. I came to a crossroads and went across it. There was a gate that led to a run-down church. I walked through the gate and went into the church and saw pews full of ghosts, just sitting there. I moved forward and at the altar was a figure like you see of death or the ferryman. I said, "I want to receive something that will help me move forward."
>
> "Okay, what have you got for me?" An orb appeared in my hands and there was a big murmur through the crowd of ghosts. I understood that I was to hand this over. I did so and the figure moved aside and let me go through.
>
> Everything turned dark. I asked my spirits to help me. I have three spirits that always come to me when something big is happening. They came, surrounded me, and persuaded me that it would be okay. "This is something big, but we are here and will look after you." They have never let me down before, so I moved on through.
>
> I moved toward a light at the end of the blackness. There was a boat; we got in and floated though reeds before bumping into solid land. They said, "Something scary may happen that you need to do. Take a step and move forward."
>
> We came to a large castle hewn out of rock and walked in through a small door. Nobody was inside. I went down to the dungeons. There was a woman in the corner of

the darkest, deepest dungeon, dressed in dark clothes. As soon as I saw her, I realized it was me. I knew what it was straight away; I knew what it referred to.

We just sat together with my spirit guides and cried, then cuddled each other. I tried to get her to come back but couldn't. I asked my teacher to do a soul retrieval for me. He took the part and blew it into me and sealed it in. I could feel the difference; I could feel it go in and settle. We went back over the river and ended up at the crossroads and said goodbye.

Journey to Discover the Collective Destiny of Humans

We have our own destinies, which are individual threads in a larger tapestry that is the collective destiny of all humans. This journey to this tapestry is to learn about our collective human destiny.

Sophia

This one was quite grim. The destiny can still be shaped. There is a way of changing course. What I got is it will go one of two ways, but the way it is going is quite grim. There was a vision of the ocean and it looked like fish, but it wasn't—it was drowning people. There was a destiny where there was more balance, and the message was it is whether humanity can overcome the obsession with materialism and step beyond that.

Pro Tips

The following tips are provided:

1. **Preparation.** As work like soul retrieval is recommended prior to destiny retrieval, it is not a modality to use with new clients unless they have done prior relevant work.

2. **Integration.** A person can journey to learn work needed or to get guidance on how they need to develop, and the life choices needed so that this destiny can be realized. Making artwork to represent a destiny helps with its integration.

3. **Destiny retrieval during soul retrieval.** A practitioner being directed to the upper world in a soul retrieval is one way in which destiny retrieval can occur.

4. **Soul retrieval during destiny retrieval.** Conversely, soul retrieval may be performed during a destiny retrieval ritual, a part being needed for us to fulfill our destiny.

5. **Fulfilling our destiny.** What happens when you fulfill our destiny? You start a new one.

PSYCHOPOMP

When people die their spirit usually goes to an upper or lower world location but can become stuck in the middle world as a ghost. Psychopomp helps stuck human (and non-human) spirits to reach their destination in the upper or lower world. Psychopomp is also a noun that describes a human or spirit that undertakes psychopomp. The psychopomp helps a spirit understand where they are, performs healing and counseling, and helps the spirit get to their preferred destination in the upper or lower world. It is possible to perform mass psychopomp on multiple spirits at the same time.

There are many examples of psychopomps in mythology, including Death, the Egyptian god Anubis, the Islamic angel of death Azrael, the Greek ferryman of the river Styx Charon, the Greek goddess Hecate, the Greek god Hermes, the Archangel Michael, the Roman god Mercury, and the Norse Valkyries. Dogs and birds are often associated with psychopomp. The psychopomp archetype also appears in literature, films, and other media.

One thing we should do is to avoid becoming a stuck ghost ourselves and ensure a smooth transition to the afterlife. We do this by celebrating our lives as we prepare to die, being fully reconciled in our relationships with others, experiencing death peacefully as a transition, and knowing that spirits will help us at death to transition if needed.

Why Spirits Become Stuck

So why do spirits become stuck in the middle world? A spirit may be in shock or confused and not know it is dead, especially if a person died suddenly. They may be preoccupied with what they are doing or attached to their life and unwilling to move on if they want to continue addictive or obsessive behaviors, look after the living, have unfinished business, or resent their life. There may be embarrassed about actions in life, feel guilty if they committed suicide, or have negative views about the afterlife. They may not know that spirits can help them.

A spirit may be being held captive. It is unlikely that you will encounter this situation, but you may be concerned about these spirits. Other work is done to help them. Nobody is left behind.

Psychopomp Indications

Psychopomp may be performed at locations where the dead are likely to be. It may also be performed in conjunction with other healing, for example as part of ancestral healing on an ancestor, as part of depossession work, or escorting non-human spirits such as animal and plant spirits to where they should go.

Psychopomp Benefits

Spirits helped by psychopomp are able to move on to their next stage. It is in everybody's interest that these spirits are helped. A ghost may affect surviving family members and even descendants by causing illness or issues such as prolonged grief, or by their energy overshadowing the living. Psychopomp removes this influence. Other living people may be affected by the presence of ghosts. There are more stuck spirits now than there were historically due to people not living and dying well, so this is becoming an increasing problem.

A psychopomp can also help the dying and their family and friends prepare for death, explaining what will happen, alleviating fear, and helping family members deal with grief.

Psychopomp Process

You journey to find a spirit who needs help or may encounter such a spirit in work such as ancestral healing. Engage in dialogue with the spirit to find out what is going on and determine if they know where they are. Compare their current state with a preferred future state, pointing out tactfully that they are dead and need to move on if necessary. You have to obtain permission from the spirit to help them. If the spirit gives permission for you to help them you then find out where the spirit would like to go, either the upper world or lower world, take them to the location in one of these worlds that the souls of dead humans go to, and then hand to over to one or more spirits who will be waiting to meet them.

You may need to perform other healing work prior to psychopomp itself or help prepare the spirit to be escorted to where they should go.

Key Ritual: Journey to Perform Psychopomp Healing

The intention is to look for the spirit of a dead person who is stuck in the middle world and who needs help to be escorted to where they should be in the upper or lower worlds.

Hilary

I asked the eagle to take me to where I was needed. I found myself in a hospital with cream and green walls. The scene was a brutal one and, helpfully for me, presented in soft focus. I could make out a woman lying on her back; however, my attention was drawn to the bottom half of her.

A necessary medical intervention had just been performed and there was a pool of blood on the bed between her legs. The baby had not survived. Despite this, I felt somewhat emotionless and detached viewing from the middle world.

As I watched a small spirit form began to lift from where the doctor's hands were working. The spirit was in great distress and I received strong messages that the baby had not expected to die as "this was not the original plan."

I reached out, drawing the spirit to me, and cradled it in my arms. I gently told it that I could help and take it to a happier and safer place. It quickly relaxed and agreed, indicating it wanted to go "up" rather than "down." Together we sped up a white, ethereal ladder to the higher planes. The destination gleamed in front of us, a shining white castle with never-ending walls.

I slowly walked with the baby toward the tall entrance gates that swung open in welcome. A pair of what can only be described as ghostly arms emerged and drawn toward the intense light, I carefully handed over the baby spirit. The ghostly arms folded themselves around the spirit and withdrew as the gates silently shut. Feelings of delight filled my being.

At this moment I became fascinated and awestruck as I realized I had been at the gates of what Christians would call heaven, and my arms had actually entered heaven and been bathed in the white light as I had passed the baby spirit through the gates. They looked and felt no different, but I knew they had been exposed to something that the rest of me had not. I also knew that this was an important step in my spiritual development.

How to Do the Key Ritual

You should first do a preparatory journey to see the locations in the lower and upper worlds that dead human spirits go to. This is described below. When you know how to reach the location in the lower and upper worlds that you will escort the spirits of the dead to, you can perform psychopomp itself.

Find a spirit that you can perform psychopomp on. This spirit will be in the middle world (if they had fully crossed over to where they are supposed to go on death they would already be in the lower or upper world). Journey to where you are guided to go or ask a helping spirit to take you to a spirit that needs help.

You might look for spirits in location they are likely to be found, such as hospitals, scenes of war and violence, scenes of disasters and accidents, or places associated with addictions and crime. Note that spirits may not necessarily be easily found in hospices, where they have a chance to prepare for death, or cemeteries. Spirits tend to be attached more to the place where they died. You can call out to ask if there is any spirit that needs help, which may attract one or more spirits to you.

If you encounter multiple spirits who need help, you have to psycho-pomp them individually, as they must express a preference of whether they want to go. Later you will see a way to do mass psychopomp if large numbers of spirits are involved.

Having found a spirit, talk to them to find out about them and about their state, convince them that you can help them, get permission from them to perform healing, and establish a preference for where they want to go to the upper or lower world (often referred to by a spirit simply as "up" or "down").

Spirits are often confused so ask questions to help them understand what happened, such as: "How are you?", "Do you know where you are?" and "Do you know what happened?" If a spirit is in distress, ask "What is wrong?" and if confused ask "What is the last thing you remember?" This helps trigger memories of what happened just prior to death.

Do not though let them focus too much on their prior life though, as you do not want them to become too attached to it. If necessary, point out to them firmly but gently that they are dead, and reiterate that you can help them if they would like (which invites them to give you permission to do the healing).

If you do not immediately get their attention or permission to perform psychopomp, use the tactic or comparing their current state with a preferred future one. Ask questions like: "Are you happy here?", "Do you know you can be in a better place?" and "Would you like me to help you?" (again, inviting permission). If the spirit wants to stay to look after others, convince them they can help if they complete their transition to where they should go, after which they will have more wisdom and power. Stress to a spirit that they will be in a better place and able to meet loved ones or others who will help them, as well as be able to help others.

Shift the focus from negative aspects the spirit has of themselves to positive aspects or to others (such as ancestors or other deceased family members of friends of the spirit). Promise benefits that the spirit will get on fully crossing over.

Provide healing such as soul retrieval if needed to help in preparation for psychopomp itself and having obtained permission from the spirit to do this as well of course. Do such healing as you would do it in physical reality or as you are otherwise guided or advised to perform it in spiritual reality. You may sense a change in color of the spirit, which is a sign they are ready to be psychopomped. This could be from a dark to a light color, or a reduction in a color associated with an emotion, such as red for anger.

If a spirit agrees that they want to be helped, ask them if they have a preference to go up or down (to the upper world or lower world). We may think that a spirit would not understand this question, but they always express a preference for a direction.

In advanced work (especially when dealing with non-human spirits) other destinations may be mentioned. You should not experience this, but if you do then you may have to think on your feet and enlist the aid of a helping spirit to take the spirit to their preferred destination.

A number of approaches may be needed to get a spirit to agree that they need to be helped, to give you permission to help them, to do other preparatory work needed, and to obtain their desired destination. At all times act with caring and compassion and give the impression that you can help and are willing to help the spirit concerned.

Be patient if the work takes longer than you expect, but do not persist if it seems that you will not be successful, or if the spirit becomes distressed by the process described. You can always set an intention to go back to them in a subsequent journey to see if you are able to help them at that point. Often an initial contact and time to reflect enables successful subsequent psychopomp healing work with a spirit.

If you get permission to do the work and have obtained their preferred destination, take the spirit by the hand, or as guided, and escort them to the lower or upper world location that you learned of. There are usually one or more spirits waiting at the destination to receive a spirit being psychopomped. Hand the spirit over to them.

One of your helping spirits may do some or all the above work. Ancestral helping spirits or other helping spirits of the spirit that you are trying to help may also assist you in the work.

Do not merge with the spirit of a deceased person who has not crossed over, as they are a ghost and are potentially a danger to you if you tried to do this. If you have a power animal or other helping spirit with you, they will intervene to prevent this.

Other Rituals

Other rituals that you can perform include: journey to meet a helping spirit for psychopomp, journey to see locations the dead go to in the lower and upper worlds, journey to learn how to do mass psychopomp, and journey to perform mass psychopomp.

Other rituals that you could perform include getting a ritual to prevent the dead from returning or getting a ritual to protect you from the dead.

Journey to Meet a Helping Spirit for Psychopomp

The intention is to journey to meet a spirit to get guidance on how to prepare for or do psychopomp. This could be an existing power animal or helping spirit, or a new spirit you only work with for this modality. If you meet a spirit, introduce yourself, and ask for any guidance they have for you. Thank any spirit that helped you and return.

> *Sue*
>
> I went to somebody I have seen before. She came out of a forest; she is dark and goes with a horseman. She is like a cross between a spider and a bat. She advised me to work in areas that had a lot of dead people and suggested it would be helpful to do psychopomp work at a full moon and to have a fire. I could work alone or with a group.

Journey to Where the Dead Go in the Lower and Upper Worlds

The intention is to travel to the locations in the lower and upper worlds the spirits of the dead go to, so that you will know where to take spirits when they have expressed a preference for where they want to go. You may not be able to enter the locations as a threshold guardian may stop you. This can be taken as one or two journeys. The location in the lower or upper world may of course look differently to the practitioner and a spirit being psychopomped.

Journey to where you are guided to go or ask the spirit that you met in the first journey, or a power animal or another or your helping spirits, to take you to see these locations. Once you have been to the lower and upper world locations concerned you will be able to return to them more quickly and easily in the future. Thank any spirit that helped you and return.

Siobhan

> In the upper world, there was a beautiful lady. The
> entrance was like a triangular stone doorway and I saw
> a hand taking a child. When that happened there was a
> sensation in my stomach. The lower world one was more
> difficult to find. It was like a wooden door and there was a
> man like a warrior standing there with a face like a wolf.

Journey to Learn How to do Mass Psychopomp

The intention is to take a journey to learn how to perform mass psychopomp. Journey to a relevant helping spirit to find out how to do this. It is
important to remember that you still need to obtain permission from individuals, to elicit their preferred destination, and to provide a way for relevant sets of spirits to go to either the lower or upper world.

Ryan

> I went to Michael. He was holding a sword. I asked him
> how to do mass psychopomp. He said, "Announce 'I am
> here to help you all to go to a better place, I need your
> permission and you can do this by stepping forward' and
> entities who give permission will move forward." They
> must let go of what ties them. I can cut ties by moving in
> a circular motion with a sword or my arm and people will
> then be released to go where they choose to go.
>
> Michael said I can also make a circle on the ground and
> when the people step into it, they give permission, and it
> also cuts their ties. I can then escort them. I can take all
> those who want to go to the lower or upper world together
> in two groups.

Journey to Perform Mass Psychopomp

Having learned how to perform mass psychopomp we now perform the
healing itself using the method that was obtained in the previous journey.

Ludivine

> It was at night and I was in a clearing. There was a fire and
> a column of white light. There was forest all around and

I could see souls coming who were attracted to the light. When they were all around, I told them you will be in a better place. I showed them images. I showed them love and could feel my heart bursting with love and joy for them. Physically I could really feel it, it was nice. I told them to separate in two groups: one to go to the underworld and one to the upper world.

We went first to the upper world. I took the first one and they were all following so we are all one big group of people. They went up and some hands took them. When I arrived in the underworld, there was nobody, but there was a mirror like water. They went inside it.

I went back to the clearing and saw there were a lot of forest animals like rabbits, mouse, rats, squirrels, small animals that wanted to come as well. I said, "Okay my darlings, who wants to go upward?" and I did the same thing. It was very nice.

Pro Tips

The following tips are provided:

1. **Belief system.** Use aspects of a spirit's belief system such as clothing or objects to make them comfortable (in spiritual reality you can intend to manifest relevant items). You can also shape-shift yourself into a form appropriate to their belief system.

2. **Preparation.** Help the spirit prepare if this helps, perhaps by cleaning and dressing them. Use praise to address low self-esteem if relevant.

3. **Messages.** We may be given messages from the dead for the living. We should pass these on only if they are positive and serve a healing purpose for the living.

4. **Disguise.** Psychopomps often disguise themselves to avoid being overwhelmed by suffering spirits in the middle world.

5. **Captive spirits.** It is unlikely you will encounter a captive spirit, which are dealt with in more advanced work. If you do it is recommended

that you do not try to intervene. Do not intend to hurt in any way an abducting spirit, who may need help themselves.

ANCESTRAL HEALING

We live in a web of relationships with different types of ancestors. As well as biological ancestors we have past life, spiritual, and vocational ancestors. Spiritual ancestors can be thought of as a spiritual family. Vocational ancestors include a tradition you belong to, which might relate to an occupation or calling such as being an artisan or an artist.

We may be in a relationship with spirits who protect a group of people we are descended from, or even such spirits that look after others if we have migrated to a place where their descendants live. Here we will focus mainly on biological ancestral healing. You can also work with descendants (even if you do not have children you still have non-biological descendants).

There are a large number of ancestors (and descendants). If we go back ten generations, there are more than a thousand biological ancestors and going back twenty generations, more than a million. This creates two problems. You cannot practically work with all of these people individually. You have to work with groups of ancestors by clearing patterns from the whole line. The other problem is that you cannot get permission from all affected people to perform such work; ancestral healing is thus in some sense intentional sorcery.

Causes of Ancestral Issues

Ancestors can provide wisdom, guidance, and healing but can cause problems for descendants. This may be due to being stuck in the middle world as ghosts, repressing behavior in a family creating a family shadow, resenting the living, or creating energy patterns that adversely affect descendants. The latter can cause physical, emotional, and mental problems. They may be embedded in land, property, or objects, causing issues including fertility problems.

Ancestors may resent the living due to being unacknowledged or ignored by descendants, or by descendants committing breaches of customs or taboos, or doing things that ancestors disagree with, such as selling land. Adoption, migration, and broken relationships may cause issues, as may people unacknowledged by a family such as illegitimate children and mistresses.

Ancestors stuck in the middle world as ghosts can be helped by psychopomp. Ancestors may also need to be healed via other healing modalities as part of removing a negative energy pattern from an ancestral line, which heals the past, present and future at the same time. Ancestors not stuck in the middle world may return as *Ancestral Helping Spirits* and help us to heal other ancestors.

Our ancestors practised rituals for the dying and lived and died without leaving unresolved issues. They were thus less likely to become stuck as ghosts or pass negative energy patterns to descendants. This is not the case now, where there are an increasing number of ghosts and unhelpful ancestral energy patterns which overshadows the living. You should try to resolve issues in your own life before death to minimize the chance of contributing to this.

Ancestral Healing Indications

Indicators negative energy patterns are being passed down an ancestral line include behavior like addictions, abuse, suicide, or breaches of taboos. Other indicators are patterns of fertility or birth issues, families breaking up or not observing traditions, or early onset of age-related illnesses. Where life or career choices are influenced by a family, descendants may feel they are not following their true calling. There may also be issued associated with land or property.

It is important to view ancestor's actions compassionately, without judgment, and forgive them. Ancestral healing can be difficult, especially if it involves historic abuse.

Ancestral Healing Benefits

Ancestral healing helps ancestors and releases energy patterns that have a negative effect on you and your descendants. This can lead to improved relationships with ancestors, help spirits release ancestral karma, and help you live your life purpose. Working with ancestral helping spirits allows this work to be more effective. The more we address our own ancestral issues the more we also remove the collective burden of unresolved ancestral energy from humanity.

Ancestral Healing Process

In general, you should build a relationship with ancestors. You can research your family tree, talk to living ancestors, build ancestral altars or shrines where you make culturally appropriate offerings, and dedicate the benefit of residual energy raised during rituals to ancestors. You can heal unresolved issues, clear ancestral patterns, and work with ancestral helping spirits. Ancestors may provide you with wisdom, power, or healing and help you live your life purpose.

Ancestral altars should be located in a space that can be closed, like a cupboard or box. Open the altar at the start of day, work with the ancestors by talking or journeying to them and close the altar at the end of day. On an altar you can place photographs and ancestral artefacts, and ritual objects like candles. An ancestral shrine can be as a home for one or more spirits.

The key to clearing patterns is to persuade the ancestor responsible for them to change the decisions and actions that created a pattern and make a different choice. If you explain the results of actions taken and the benefits of changes, most ancestors are willing to help. Ancestral spirits may need other healing such as soul retrieval or psychopomp, which you can perform for them. When an issue is resolved, you and/or helping spirits clear the energetic pattern created from its source to the present, preventing it being passed to descendants.

Ancestral helping spirits want to help us and will do so if you ask for assistance. You can ask them to help us heal ancestors and create other ancestral helping spirits. You can also ask them to take you to meet a group of ancestral helping spirits who can offer advice and healing.

Key Ritual: Journey to Heal One of Your Ancestors with a Helping Spirit

The intention is to journey with a helping spirit to perform healing on one of your ancestors. This could be a spirit that helps you with ancestral healing, or an ancestral helping spirit.

Lucie

It was sad and beautiful at the same time. The helping spirit and I fly together. We arrived, it is winter, it is snowing, it is cold. There is a small house and a woman crying, really crying badly. Then there is a horse with a carriage, and I understand she had to give away her baby. I can see the baby is crying, the mum is crying, and the dad is trying to pull away the mother so that she can't get the baby, as the baby has to leave. So, maybe, it's like they sold the baby or something.

We look at the scene and I say, "The horse will not leave."

The helping spirit says, "This is what you think?"

I say, "Yes, because we are here the horse will not leave."

The horse starts leaving and after a few steps it stops. So, the mum gets the baby, and the father says "No, we need to put it back."

Then there is another round of crying and stuff. The horse starts again but stops again. It is not going anywhere. The mum realized she has a window of opportunity to get her baby back because the horse is not going anywhere. "I can get my baby back; I will get it now."

So, she gets the baby back and the husband is trying to reason with her, "We cannot afford it, we cannot do that."

She says, "No, it is going to be fine, we need to trust that there I something higher that will help us to keep the baby."

After that we journeyed to another scene where I can see the baby has grown up and it is between spring and summertime. The kid is older, still a toddler, but is really joyful because there is lots of sun. It is in the middle of a rice field, and you get the impression that it was fine because they just planted more. There is another kid as well. It is two girls. So, they have not only kept the first baby.

How to Do the Key Ritual

You should first do a preparatory journey before you do the key journey. This can be to meet a spirit who may give you advice about and/or help you with this healing modality, or it could be to meet one of your ancestral helping spirits. Examples of both journeys are provided.

The intention is to journey to an ancestor who is the source of an energetic pattern or issue to heal them and/or resolve an issue or trauma they are responsible for. You may see how energetic patterns or issues manifest in your life and clear a pattern or issues.

When an issue is resolved, you and/or helping spirits clear the energetic pattern created from its source to the present, removing the energy from intervening generations and preventing it from being passed to descendants.

You might do this by visualizing the ancestral line as a tube and flush negative energy from this by blowing into or putting energy into the end of the tube that is in the past. Intend that the entire ancestral line is cleared of this energy, including future generations. You might also enlist the help of your power animal(s) and other helping spirits to assist you with this.

Other Rituals

Other rituals that you can perform include: journey to meet a helping spirit for ancestral healing, journey to meet an ancestral helping spirit, journey to heal an ancestor, journey to learn to construct and use an ancestral altar or shrine, journey to meet an ancestral council, journey to meet your spirit family, and journey to perform ancestral healing for another person.

Journey to Meet a Helping Spirit for Ancestral Healing

The intention is to journey to meet a spirit to get guidance on how to prepare for or do ancestral healing. This could be an existing power animal or helping spirit, or a new spirit you only work with for this modality. If you meet a spirit, introduce yourself, and ask for any guidance they have for you.

Lisa

I ended up at an antechamber with lots of drawers. Within these are souls which can help us in our learning. I chose a drawer, and a lovely old fellow came out who looked like he was from Elizabethan times. I said I had come to ask him if he could give me lessons and guidance about healing ancestors and he said "Yes, of course. I am going to show you the mountain of ancestors; you need to start at the top." He took me up to the top of this huge mountain.

He said "If you look down, humanity starts here, and it goes down. You need to find your own trace of humanity, your own ancestors. As you follow you can see what goes down each thread of ancestry. Sometimes it is blood and tears and sometimes it is cut. There is often a break. There are all sorts of connections. Find your own line, or whatever ancestral line you are helping, and start going down that line and look until you find someone that needs help."

He continued, "When you find someone, ask what you need to do to help, what has happened, and offer to help. As you are asking to help them, they can say they want help or decline. Provide healing and go on down the mountain. You have to find where the problem is, where there is a break in the path or where there is energy that indicates healing is needed."

It was very visual, very interesting. It felt like I was going back to the ice age in the ancestry from this life. He said, "You can go anywhere, the most important thing is you identify where you need to go." It is giving me a three-dimensional map.

I asked, "How do you know when something is healed?"

"You dont know; you just have to try your best."

"What about in my line? What do I look for?"

"There are lots of battles in your line, there's lots of fighting."

"Maybe I do not want to be a warrior or to battle."

"Well, maybe that is what you need to heal."

"Can I come back and learn from you again?"

"Yes, of course you can."

Journey to Meet an Ancestral Helping Spirit

The intention is to journey to meet an ancestral helping spirit to get to know them and how you will work with them. You could then ask this spirit to help you heal another ancestor, as in the key ritual. You may also receive a healing from an ancestral helping spirit.

Salina

I went to a marketplace where I met my ancestor, a man who was quite old with gray hair and a hat like the one a Moroccan man would wear. He didn't look Arabic to me, more Jewish. He took me on his donkey, and we went through plains to really high cliffs. I saw two ancestors.

One was in a cave doing witchcraft. He looked really dark with evil eyes, not a nice person to be around, but I didn't get to that one. The other one who originally was a shepherd was dressed in black and was a thief. My ancestor spirit talked to him and said if he kept doing what he did he would be caught and killed and tried to show him the sort of life he could alternatively have. He started crying and the ancestral helping spirit healed him by pouring some water over him.

Journey to Heal an Ancestor

In this journey the intention is to journey on your own to heal one of your ancestors.

Ryan

I went to the underworld, got on my power animal and we went to a cemetery where my grandfather is buried. I got off and said, "Your grandson is here to heal you." The grave opened up and he stepped out. He died of cancer. I didn't know him well or what emotional stuff caused the cancer. We talked about why he was a hard man. He was a carpenter. Once he cut the tip off his finger and just bandaged it up and kept going saying he had a lot to do. That's the kind of man he was.

He was quite hard to my father. I asked why. He said stuff
I already knew which was to do with the war. He was one
of the first people on the beach in Micronesia and then
was missing in action. He had anger from that. He said
you don't need to know any more. He asked how I would
heal him. I said by giving him a hug from his grandson
and with love.

I wanted to draw the anger out of him and merged
with my power animal. We had a hug, and he gave me
his anger. Then my animal and I went at a frantic pace,
because of the anger energy, to a location with fields,
water and the mountains. I got off and the horse blew the
anger out of his nose. I had the intention that it was to
disperse and be transformed.

Journey to Learn to Construct and Use an Ancestral Altar or Shrine

The intention is to find out how to create an ancestral altar or shrine and
work with ancestors, including what offerings to use. If your family emi-
grated decide whether to use your original ancestry and/or ancestors of
where you live. An ancestral altar or shrine is usually inside as you typically
work with it on a daily basis. Ancestors can be consulted about the design,
construction and consecration of altars or shrines, and involved in consecration rituals to activate and energise altars or shrines.

Ryan

One side of my family is from Scotland. For the altar, I
am to get tartan cloth. My grandfather was a carpenter so
I will get a carpenter's tool, coal, a bit of hawthorn, and
photos of ancestors alive since I was born, back to my
grandfather.

Journey to Meet an Ancestral Council

The intention is to journey to ask an ancestral helping spirit, or other spirit,
to take you to meet an ancestral council, a group of ancestors that can offer
healing and advice.

Salina

There were chairs in a circle and I saw some ancestors, Arab, Jewish, and Black. The message I got was to try to see beyond differences and understand we are all one and the same. Wherever I go I will find home, I must rediscover my roots. I should go back and change my point of view, which is negative about my heritage. There are some things in my culture I have rejected, and I need to revisit that.

Journey to Meet Your Spirit Family

The intention in this journey is to go to meet your spirit family. You should be open as to who will be in your family. It may be spirits that you have already met in previous journeys, or you may realize that you have a large spirit family, most of whom you have not yet met. People sometimes find that they do not want to leave their spirit family and return from this journey.

Lucie

It seems that my spirit ancestor is from my spirit family. I am in a Native American setting. There are people that I do not know. She says, "We are all the same family, maybe you do not remember everyone, but everybody knows you."

Then we go in a circle and she tells me I need to help connect things, because once we connect things, we build power. Then, in the small circle we are in (although maybe not that small as I did not see everybody in that circle) we create huge fields of energy, spiraling and beautiful. Then I see my daughter coming. She is casual about it; she knows where she is going, and she comes into the circle to help us. During the journey, my spirit gave me something for me daughter. It is a charm. It looks like a snowflake but inside is the sun. I say it is very pretty, what is it for. She says it is for luck and protection. I am supposed to pass it to her.

We do that for quite a while and then she tells me there are lots of things I need to learn and digest, but everything comes when I am ready, so I don't need to worry about the timing.

Then the group walks, and we encounter a big group of black buffalos. We show respect. It is beautiful. Then one of them jumps into me. I ask, "Why do I need one more power animal?" She says, "It might not be for full action now; it is more for strength and persistence and it will help when it is needed."

She says there are more members to meet that I have seen before in the upper world; the family is much bigger. When I hear the drum for the callback I realize that I haven't seen how big this family is. When I first started the circle, I had the impression it was fairly small, but when you were calling us back, they started showing themselves and there were lots of them everywhere. I asked, "How many people are there?" She said, "You do not need to know now, we are watching what you are doing, but you do not need to worry about that."

Lucie can pass the charm to her daughter in the same way that a power animal is given to a person after it has been retrieved, explaining that it is to bring luck and protection. She could also have passed it to her directly in the journey.

Journey to Perform Ancestral Healing for Another Person

The intention is to journey to heal an ancestor and, if necessary, clear the line of negative energetic patterns.

Dawn

I saw a cave and there's a child. It is an ancient time. This child is alone, and she is lonely. She is going to pass at that moment. I talked to her and cuddled her and got my ancestral helping spirits and dragon, and a little bird, to perform a kind of wrap around her and help her to pass, to remove loneliness while the little bird is singing.

Lisa

I am looking for an ancestor of yours. I am in a big forest.
There's a stream, very fast running, and there is a really
ancient tribe living there. There is a little old lady who is
very upset. It is like the tribe is casting her out for doing
something. I go up to the lady. I ask what is it that has
happened, why are you so upset. She is upset with the
tribe and the tribe is upset with her. They have done something she does not agree with.

They have killed a sacred animal and disturbed sacred
ground and upset spirits. She has kicked up a hell of a fuss.
They have disturbed their ancestors. I am asking what I
can do to help. She is so hurt that they have rejected her,
it's like they have turned their back on her, and she is feeling very isolated. She needs to find a way back to the tribe.
She needs somebody to talk to them so they can forgive
each other. She also needs to forgive them.

The tribe is moving on and leaving her behind. They are
ignoring her. "What do you need?" She needs to make
reparation to the spirits so there can be forgiveness of
her tribe, and then the tribe will go on and she will be at
peace. I feel that we need to make a sacrifice to tree spirits.
We go to a big tree and we make a sacrifice; we bury something for the tree spirits and ask forgiveness. We ask that
this old lady gets forgiveness, and her tribe gets forgiveness. Then she is released.

She has to let them go and remain behind, but she is
happy that the tree spirits have forgiven them, and she
knows that they will be okay. I ask my power animals to
come in and clear any residual hatred back to her and
between her and the tribe so the tribe can continue in a
healthy way and not upset the spirits again. She is much
more at peace now.

Pro Tips

The following tips are provided:

1. **Separation.** Maintain a clear divide between the living and dead. The only work we do with ancestors stuck as ghosts is healing such as psychopomp.

2. **Ancestral altars and shrines.** Do not represent the living on an ancestral altar or shrine. This is inviting the living to join the ancestors!

3. **Calling in ancestors.** We should invoke ancestral helping spirits at the start of ceremonies and not just ancestors, which may invite ghosts to be present.

4. **Adoption.** If you are adopted, you can work with biological lineage (even if you do not know who they are) and/or the lineage of your non-biological parents.

5. **Think big.** Do not work on small issues, but on those where there is potential to heal a large number of people and make a significant contribution to humanity in general.

CHAPTER 3

NATURE

You are connected to nature and nature spirits, and use animal and plant products for food, fuel, clothes, medicine, and building materials. Human activities may disturb nature spirits and affect people, animals, and crops. You can work with nature and nature spirits to restore balance and harmony. You can work with spirits of nature in a number of ways, including:

- Honoring ancestral helping spirits (even if not our own) and other nature spirits.

- Performing animal ceremonies and rituals to ask for success in hunting and fishing.

- Performing plant ceremonies and rituals to protect crops or ask for a good harvest.

- Healing animal or plant spirits and other nature spirits.

- Healing land damaged by human activities, pollution, or global warming.

- Remedying transgressions made by humans.

- Reconciling relationships to establish and maintain balance and harmony.

Types of Spirits of Nature

There are several different nature spirits, with some overlap between categories:

- The earth (or Gaia).

- Regional guardian spirits such as spirits of mountain ranges, rivers, or old forests.

- Local guardian spirits such as spirits of individual mountains, waterfalls, or trees.

- Spirits associated with sacred sites like wells or springs.

- Forces of nature such as storms.

- Elemental beings.

- Fairies.

- Ancestral spirits who choose to reincarnate into features of the landscape.

- Spirits of man-made artefacts in the landscape like cities, power lines, or roads.

- Archetypal spirits that look after animals, plants and minerals.

- Spirits of individual animals, plants and minerals.

Natural Product Regulations

You should be aware of regulations governing export, import, and use of animal or plant parts or products, including the Convention on International Trade in Endangered Species of Wild Fauna and Flora (CITES), the USA Endangered Species Act, the EU Wildlife Trade Regulations, and the UK Control of Trade in Endangered Species (Enforcement) Regulations. Many species are protected, and it is illegal to possess parts, including most wild bird feathers.

Sourcing Natural Products

Try to ensure that animal or plant parts or products are not obtained from inappropriate sources, especially if this involves abuse of animals. You do not want to create a demand for animal or plant parts that encourages such abuse or endangerment. Buy items from reputable individuals and understand how the part or product was sourced. In some cases, you can only procure items indirectly, but then you should be able to ascertain that a vendor is reputable from advertising, and policy statements published on their website.

Pro Tips

The following tips are provided:

1. **Ancestor spirits.** Due to people being moved off ancestral land and migrations, the ancestor spirits that we work with may or may not be our own ancestors.

2. **Local spirits.** A spirit may be present even if an object it looked after no longer exists, such as the spirit of an old forest where the forest disappeared from the landscape.

3. **Nature spirits.** Spirits of nature can be disrupted by human activities, conflict, or damage to the environment. Some locations are not appropriate for humans to live in. Given the history of exploitation and destruction of nature, humans are often not trusted by nature spirits, and you may have to earn their trust.

4. **Correspondences.** Correspondences for aspects of nature like trees, herbs, and crystals vary. Seek to understand your personal symbology and correspondences.

5. **Offerings.** When making offerings in nature use natural items that decompose like tobacco and vegetable foodstuffs, rather than man-made items like coins.

ANIMALS

There are individual animal spirits, spirits that look after or represent a species, and spirits that look after animals (especially game animals), the latter usually referred to by terms like *The Keeper of the Animals*. Ways you can work with animals include:

- Animal communication and healing
- Working with the Keeper of the Animals
- The Wild Hunt
- Tracking and hunting
- Understanding animal migrations

Many shamanic tools are traditionally made of animal parts, such as hide used in a drum or decorative components such as feathers. Animal parts are also sometimes used in rituals, such as use of feathers of fans in clearing or use of animal bones in divination. These can often be replaced with non-animal materials.

Animal Communication and Healing

Animal communication is used to facilitate dialogue between humans and animal companions, and to address health or behavioral issues. It can also be used prior to or following moving, placing an animal in a temporary facility, adding a pet to an existing family, or if an animal or human companion is dying or has died. Animals may also have their own reasons for wanting to communicate with us. You can work with wild animals, observing appropriate safeguards.

Normal animal communication occurs via telepathic or intuitive transfer of words, pictures, emotions, and feelings. This can be done in person or remotely. Dialogue with a companion animal can confirm if the animal is happy or wants anything, uncover issues the animal has or any problems caused, perhaps inadvertently, by humans. This may include issues with a domestic animal's diet or training. The practitioner may also perform healing on the animal.

In shamanic animal work you can journey to and work directly with an animal's spirit, or work with a helping spirit such as a power animal who acts as an intermediary with the animal. It is often suggested that you obtain permission from a human companion to do work. You may also, in addition to or instead, confirm with an animal's spirit if it wants work to be performed.

You can communicate with animals to establish a deeper relationship with your own animal companions or to deepen your understanding of the animal kingdom through communication with archetypal or individual animal spirits. You can also use animal communication as a way of removing fears and phobias of certain animals, or to agree actions that allow harmonious co-existence between humans and animals, for example with invasive species.

Shamanic animal healing can be done by a practitioner or by a spirit and involves the same modalities we use on humans, which work effectively for animals. Power animal retrieval can be used to provide a feeling of safety, abilities, strength, or power to a physical animal. A power animal such as Wolf may be retrieved for a domestic dog. Helping spirits can also advise after-healing care or other guidelines.

If an animal is dying, you can connect them to spirits they return to after death. This provides comfort and helps them prepare. You can also help humans and animals say goodbye. After an animal's death you can use psychopomp if it is stuck in the middle world or facilitate communication with the animal. This can provide comfort to a human companion that the animal is not suffering and is where it should be. You can also facilitate communication between the spirit of a human companion and an animal that is still living.

If a practitioner has been asked to intervene and, through animal communication, finds out the process that is happening is the best course for the animal and intervention is not required, they should communicate this to the human companion and not proceed with further work.

You should not do anything that interferes with medical treatment or advice that has been prescribed or provided by a veterinarian.

The Keeper of the Animals

The Keeper of the Animals is a figure, often a deity, seen in mythology. Other names for this figure include: *The Master/Mistress of the Animals* or *The Lord/Lady of the Forest*. They often have both human and animal characteristics. Examples of deities who fulfil this role are the Roman goddess Diana and Greek goddess Artemis, Goddesses of the hunt and wild animals.

The Keeper of the Animals controls and protects animals or fish and makes them available to hunters. In tribal societies, if there was a scarcity of game animals or fish, a shaman journeyed to the Keeper of the Animals to find out why and what could be done to restore game. This may involve public atonement for transgressions (often breaches of taboo). When a ritual had been held to appease the Keeper of the Animals, the hunters or fishers were again successful.

The Wild Hunt

The *Wild Hunt* is a myth involving a supernatural group of hunters, engaged in a pursuit through the night sky and forest, to accompaniment of wild winds, lightning, and thunder. The Wild Hunt varies across cultures, but there are common themes:

- The hunt's passing is marked by loud noises, e.g., pounding hooves and howling dogs.
- Associations with the dead and the underworld, cults of the dead, and warfare.
- A leader who gathers dead spirits. This is often a deity like Odin or Freya, or a person condemned to lead the hunt as a punishment for their sins.
- The hunters are supernatural beings or the dead.
- The prey is often a young (magical) woman, disembodied souls, or sinners.
- People's spirits may be unwittingly drawn into the hunt while they sleep.

The Wild Hunt was originally believed to bring blessings, but was later associated with war, disease, famine, or the death or abduction of witnesses of the hunt to the underworld. This may be due to pagan beliefs being replaced by demonized equivalents in organized religion.

Livestock Rituals

Rituals are traditionally used to protect or heal livestock herds, or to ask for abundant yields of animal products such as milk. These are often derived from folklore or folk medicine and performed at festivals which mark key points in the agricultural cycle.

You can also journey to provide protection to or heal a herd of livestock animals, either on your own or using a specialist helping spirit. If you are working with a herd, you may want to communicate with the lead animal what you intend and get their advice or permission. You can also work with fairy animals, which are often associated with physical animal herds.

Tracking and Hunting

Tracking involves recognising animal tracks and sign and understanding behavior. Animals gather where there is cover, food and water, often in transition areas between habitats such as forests, fields, and streams. Different species have distinctive tracks. You can also track using signs such as dens, feeding areas, places animals rub or scratch things, or droppings.

Hunting cultures have strong ties with game animals and many rituals associated with hunting. You can adapt these to your own use. The following are some typical hunting rituals: journeying to a spirit that looks after animals, to obtain permission to hunt, journeying to find the location of animals (a traditional role of the shaman), pre-hunt rituals like purification, prayers, and preparation of hunters and weapons, during the hunt praying to winds, rivers, mountains, etc. for protection and success, killing animals in a ritual manner and asking forgiveness of the spirit of an animal, rituals to respect the animal's spirit, such as dressing its carcass in ceremonial clothing, and rituals to expedite the journey of the soul of the killed animal to the afterlife.

Animal Migrations

Migration is movement of animals alone or in groups between locations. Animals migrate to find food or water, avoid extreme temperature, or to reproduce, give birth to, and raise young. Migration is seen in humans, mammals, birds, fish, reptiles, amphibians, crustaceans, and insects. It is also seen in plants, where populations migrate via seed dispersal.

Whales migrate from cold to warm water for mating. Some bird species migrate, usually north to south. Fish migrate to spawn or feed, migration of salmon up rivers being a migration between saltwater and freshwater. Insects like butterflies can migrate long distances, mating on the journey so successive generations complete a migration. Long-distance migrations include the Monarch Butterfly (2,000 miles) and Sooty Shearwater (20,000 miles).

Animals are thought to navigate during migrations by tracking movement of the sun, using the positions of stars, detecting the earth's magnetic field to locate north and south, or using landscape features such as mountain ranges, rivers or coastlines as a map.

Key Ritual: Journey to Perform Animal Communication and Healing

The intention is to journey to meet an animal and communicate with it and/or heal it.

Sophia

I communicated with my French Bulldog. His name is Duke. It was quite difficult because it felt like communicating to a child; there was little in the way of applied logic. We communicated but there were a lot of unresolved issues. It felt like having a conversation with a child. You can't rationalise, you can only incentivize. I thought it was communicating though.

We agreed that he would be less stubborn on walks if I were to reward him with small treats. He looks at me and doesn't walk and leans back. We didn't resolve the licking. He licks his paws from itchiness. He can't help himself. Why doesn't he express himself? He doesn't express himself because he doesn't know how to. He told me his cone is a bit annoying, he doesn't like that being put on. When he moved home it was a bit traumatic for him; we had a chat about that. I didn't get to the flatulence.

How to Do the Key Ritual

Discuss the ritual with a human companion if you are working with a domestic animal. Find out if you will work with the animal directly or an intermediary spirit. You can ask a helping spirit to accompany you and give advice on this, and also act as an intermediary. Journey to an animal's spirit with an intention to facilitate communication and perform healing if needed. Introduce yourself or ask an intermediary spirit to do so. Explain to the animal your intention and ask if they agree to communication and, if relevant, healing being provided.

If the animal agrees and gives permission, then continue to work. Otherwise, ask the animal if they would like to be asked again in the future, thank them for communicating with you, wish them well, and say goodbye to them. If you are working on behalf of a human animal companion, explain to them that the animal has requested that work not be done at this time and explain that you cannot continue without permission to do such work.

Having confirmed that you can proceed, establish communication with the animal, or via a helping spirit, and ask if the animal has anything that they want to communicate to you in general. Be open to receive communication and decide next steps based on what the animal communicates. This may be to pass a message to a human companion. Note that advanced practitioners can maintain a dialogue with a human companion while in the journey allowing interactivity with the animal in a similar way to normal animal communication.

Then ask the animal if it wants anything. Following this, confirm if there are any issues or problems that it wants to tell you about, and if it has any suggested courses of action that could be taken to address these.

Finally, ask the animal if any healing is needed. You may or may not need to explain healing options to the animal, depending on whether they have been exposed to shamanic healing modalities before. If the animal provides their permission, proceed to perform healing.

Other Rituals

Other rituals that you can perform include: journey to the Keeper of the Animals, journey to the Wild Hunt, journey to participate in hunting or tracking, journey to take part in a migration, journey to retrieve a power animal for an animal, journey to perform animal psychopomp, and journey to perform mass animal psychopomp.

You can also perform rituals to protect or heal a livestock herd via journeys or physical reality rituals, using the discussion above as a basis for the design of such rituals. An example is not included here given that this is highly specialized work that most readers will not encounter.

Journey to the Keeper of the Animals

The intention is to journey to the Keeper of the Animals to find out how to work with animals.

> #### Sam
>
> I traveled to the underworld and saw the animal keeper;
> she is half animal and half fern or moss with branches
> coming out of her head. She is golden colored and was
> feeding the deer. She says she is the animal keeper and said
> her role is to keep the cycle and balance of the environment. She is one of Mother Earth's representatives.

She said we need to learn how to respect animals and come back to living in balance and more naturally with the earth. We should not kill pregnant animals or kill unnecessarily. She says Mother Earth is working and there will be more natural disasters in the future. We will be encouraged by this to live in a right way.

Journey to the Wild Hunt

The intention is to journey to the Wild Hunt. This offers an initiation into the wild. We can witness the Hunt passing and may be taken by the Hunt (voluntarily or not).

Sue

I went to the middle world and there were a lot of people and animals running around. It was very chaotic and confusing. The Keeper of the Animals came over. I asked how I follow the Hunt and she said, "Climb on my back." We flew after the Hunt.

Beings were coming from all places, including mythical beings, converging in an area between the middle and upper world. Everybody was converging in the middle and swirling around. Then they came flying out and went off in one direction.

I asked where they were going. She said they were going to fight evil wherever it exists. I asked why is there so much evil and they said it is getting stronger, there are not enough warriors, they are lost and confused and cannot find their way here. I asked what we can do about that and she said we need to help find these souls, tell them where to go, and make them aware there is a way to move forward.

I saw the Hunt come back and there were not as many. I asked what had happened to the warriors who did not come back, and they said they fought such a strong battle that there were spread out and were dissipated. I asked what else I could do, and she said teach people from early a better way of thinking and doing things. Try to do as much as you can to prevent evil building up. If you see something that is not right speak up, don't just let it go.

Journey to Participate in Hunting or Tracking

The intention is to journey to a hunter or tracker to learn more about hunting or tracking. If we participate in a hunt this may be from the perspective or the hunter or the hunted.

Lilian

A bird of some kind came to collect me and said we needed to be above the middle world. I felt the vibration of the ground, with lots of people dancing and drumming, and when they moved it looked like it was fire. On the horizon the animals came as they called to them. There were hundreds of them and there was a surge of energy as they came down.

Among the people there was a leader who was like a god with horns. He leapt into the herd and I think he bit an animal and called to the herd for an animal to come forth that is willing to sacrifice himself for us. It seemed like there was an older fatter animal at the end and there seemed to be an understanding between the people and this animal.

The people got on their horses and created a field of confusion around the animal. The kill took a while; there was struggle and fear but also an understanding and giving. After the kill passed somebody came and did a ritual to release the animal. As they were taking the animal apart there was lot of love for the creature and a lot of respect for the sacrifice.

Journey to Take Part in a Migration

Here you journey to take part in a migration to experience it and learn about animals involved (and perhaps something about yourself). Intend to join the migration, shape-shifting into the animal concerned.

Lilian

I felt as a dragonfly I began my life in the water. I looked at the world at the surface of the water looking through water and air like wearing bifocals. I could see different shapes, tones, and flashes of color. It also felt like time was different for the dragonfly. I could feel movement and it was like they could freeze time, see a creature in slow motion, and zoom in on it.

They were constantly looking for water to sustain themselves. They flew in bursts of energy. There was sense of a vibration in the head, a buzzing. I suspected it was part of what guided them because if they veer to one side or the other it shifts subtly. We got to a muddy swampy area which was the destination.

Journey to Retrieve a Power Animal for an Animal

The intention is to journey to meet an animal, ask it is it would like a power animal retrieval and then perform this for the animal if it gives permission to do this. You might ask one of your power animals to take you to an animal that needs power animal retrieval, or journey to the spirit of an animal that you are a companion for.

Sophia

I asked Duke for permission to retrieve a power animal. He was pretty indifferent about it. I took that as a yes and retrieved a Monkey for him. The monkey was about sparking curiosity and interest. Duke is a very lazy boy. I put it into him in spiritual reality and came back and told him about it, and that he can work with it in dreams.

Journey to Perform Animal Psychopomp

The intention is to psychopomp animal spirits. Places to seek such spirits are farms and zoos.

Lilian

A gorilla was there chewing flowers and said I am going to bring you on a journey we are going to go look for Saint Francis. We found him in a monastery and then went to what looked like a military warehouse with people doing experiments on animals in cages. It was upsetting, I felt the fear. There was also an aspect where they wanted to break the mind and spirit of the animal and make them vicious.

There was a lot of confusion in the animals. After they passed their souls felt trapped. It felt intense like a dark entity that could not be released. Saint Francis said we will infuse light into the animals. I said let's go down and drive them out. He said you cannot drive them out, we have to call them to entice them out. I had a sense all I had to do was hold space while St. Francis did the work and took them into the light.

Journey to Perform Mass Animal Psychopomp

The intention is to journey to perform mass psychopomp on animals. We use techniques to gather and transport animal spirits and may be assisted by other spirits.

Ryan

There is a place in New Zealand called Kaikoura where there is a shelf close to land where whales feed. The original settlers used to slaughter whales, drag them to the shore and cut them up. There were thousands of their souls there. I drew a vertical circle they swam into, a portal, and they swam out of the middle world. As well as the whales leaving, the memory of what happened dissolved.

Pro Tips

The following tips are provided:

1. **Hunting.** When hunting animals, only kill what you eat and use every part of the animal.

2. **Taboo animals.** Some animals are taboo and not hunted, for example wolves, eagles and rattlesnakes. People generally do not kill or consume power or totem animals.

3. **Tracking.** When tracking animals, do not disturb nesting or feeding areas which may lead to young animals being abandoned. Tracks are more visible in early morning or late afternoon when the sun hits the ground at an angle, or if you keep tracks between you and a light source. Be aware of scat, poison plants, ticks, insects, and snakes.

4. **Shape-shifting.** Do not assume other forms too frequently or for too long, and be aware shape-shifting can cause you to take on energy of behavior of the form.

5. **Tricksters.** Animals such as coyote, fox and rabbit are often tricksters. This may complicate working with them, but trickster spirits can be great teachers and that they are not necessarily acting against you for the sake of it.

PLANTS

There are individual plant spirits, spirits who represent a species, and spirits that look after plants in general (especially sacred plants). Knowledge of plant medicine often comes from plant spirits. Ways you can work with plants include:

- Power plant retrieval

- Plant communication and healing

- Agricultural rituals

- Working with sacred plants

- Working with trees

• Working with herbs

Plants are used extensively in shamanic work, with incenses, oils, and plant offerings being used in rituals. You can merge with a plant spirit to empower plant remedies. You can also use plant spirits directly in healing without the physical remedies being used at all. Here we would merge with the plant spirit and pass the plant spirit's power directly to a person.

Many people prefer to grow their own plants or use wild ones rather than buying plants, to avoid ones affected by chemicals like fertilisers or pesticides. Active ingredients in plants vary based on variety, location, weather, season, time of harvest, and preparation method. Plants used for their roots should be planted and gathered at the waning moon; those used for their flowers, leaves and fruit planted and gathered at the waxing moon. Explain your intention to the plant, get permission to use it, express gratitude and make a reciprocal offering. When collecting and storing plants use paper rather than plastic bags.

Plant Communication and Healing

Communication from plants and trees may come in the form of a message, song, image, feeling, etc. It may also involve physical actions in nature involving the plant or animals. Time may be an issue, with communication taking place over a long period, or not being able to communicate with plants at certain times, e.g., during the winter when they are dormant.

Some spirits may not want to communicate, perhaps because of prior human activities, and you may need to persevere to win their trust. Some plants like to communicate with humans, especially cultivated plants, and healing herbs, but some do not resonate well with humans, such as poisonous plants. The land and individual plants and trees remember. The more you communicate with them, or are just in their presence, the more communication will come.

You may be intuitively drawn to a plant. You may want to research the physical plant or tree, and how people have worked with them in the past, especially for medicinal purposes. It helps to be able to clearly identify a plant or tree species. You can also research the mythology associated with a species and its use in rituals.

Approach a plant you are drawn to with respect and ask to communicate with it. Sit with the plant and sense how it reacts. If you feel it is open to communicate make an offering to it and sing, play music or talk to it. You may need to tend the plant in some way, such as scattering its seeds or removing pests (without harming them). Clear your mind and be open to receiving messages in whatever form. If you do not get a response try again later. Visit a plant repeatedly to build a relationship. The more you practice the more effective communication will be. You may also do this in a group and compare different messages that people receive.

You may be guided to work with a plant or pick one to work with. Preparatory work may involve dieting with it, eating or taking an infusion of it to allow you to sense and communicate with the plant spirit. Meditating with plants helps merging with a plant spirit to experience its nature. A journey can be taken to meet a plant spirit, which may not look like the physical plant (often appearing as an animal).

Power songs may be taught by plants. These are simple and may only have melody or tones but can have words. Power songs often have a specific purpose, like helping to communicate with the plant or for healing or divination. Songs are used by the person who receives them. When used in healing the healing energy is transferred to a person or other entity by singing the song into their energy body, with or without the plant being physically present.

Power Plant Retrieval

We work with power plants, spirits who may be trees, herbs or flowers. Preparatory work may be done with a plant helper prior to journeying to meet it. This can involve holding it, carrying it, meditating with it, or dieting with it to connect to and establish a relationship with the plant. A journey can be taken to find and meet the plant spirit, which may look different from the physical plant.

A power plant is retrieved by you or for another person in the same way as a power animal. If a power plant is retrieved, you can journey with the power plant or use it in rituals. A power song is often given by the power plant to you, to be used in healing work.

Agricultural Crop Rituals

Agricultural ceremonies and rituals are concerned with crop fertility or protection. The aim of rituals is divination and to appease spirits, especially those associated with crops, the spring or rain, usually via some form of sacrifice. The lunar calendar plays an important part in agricultural rituals. Activities like cultivation are undertaken in a ritual manner. Important points in the agricultural cycle include locating fields, preparing fields (for example by burning and clearing), planting, cultivation, and harvests.

A number of rituals are seen across cultures including working with crop spirits, use of offerings, using fire to clear and purify land and to produce ashes to sprinkle on fields to improve harvests, use of song and dance, wearing masks to frighten bad spirits away from fields, divination, or healing. Spirits can live in fields in spirit houses or other objects to ensure a good harvest and be sent home again afterward. Crop failures can result from crop spirits being scared or offended by rules being ignored. We can communicate with spirits to determine the cause and what needs to be done to address this.

We can use or adapt the same healing techniques used for people for plants. One example is crop soul retrieval which can be done in the same way as soul retrieval for people.

Sacred Plants

Shamans use psychoactive plants like ayahuasca to communicate with plant spirits, and for healing. These plants are referred to as sacred, teacher, or master plants. Knowledge and power come from them in the form of visions, spirit communion and merging with universal consciousness. Use of sacred plants is not necessary to do shamanic work. Sacred plants should only be used under the guidance of experienced practitioners, in a relevant setting, and probably not outside of their cultural context.

Trees

We obtain timber, food, and medicine from trees. We breathe oxygen in and carbon dioxide out; trees process carbon dioxide and make oxygen. Trees give us wisdom, serve as guardians and guides, heal, and are used as shrines or places where ceremonies are conducted.

Trees are symbols of transformation, growth, protection, and fertility, but also symbols of decay, death, resurrection, and immortality. Sacred trees are found in all traditions, especially the world tree. Trees have their roots in the earth, symbolising connection to the lower world, their trunks in the middle world, and their branches and leaves reaching to the upper world. In religions trees are sources of enlightenment, or where people sit or are crucified or hung.

Individual trees have their own spirits and there are spirits for tree species. There are also spirits (usually female) that reside in trees and act as guardians to them, called dryads or wood nymphs (dryads are technically specific to oak trees but the term is often used generically). A dryad can be seen on the surface of a tree as a face or figure. There is usually a head dryad of a forest, found near the center, and dryads guarding forest edges. Dryads are older than trees and accumulate knowledge. They move by growing trees in the direction they wish to travel.

Trees help us ground, transmute energy, empower us, help us connect with other realms, and help us to heal or to heal others. Different trees teach specific things. Introduce yourself to a tree, tell it your intentions, and ask for permission to work with it. You can also ask forest spirits to guide you to a tree to work with. Approach a tree slowly and feel its energy. Sit with your back to it and open your senses to feel it and its surroundings. Ask what it can teach or do for you and how you can help it. Trees may teach you stories or songs and like to be sung to. You can also journey to a tree in the middle world to learn how to work with it.

Prayer ribbons, pieces of fabric carrying intentions and prayers, may be tied to trees. A tie is charged with an intention and loosely tied to a branch. A prayer ribbon is empowered by nature energies like sunlight and your intention or prayer carried by the winds to spirit. Ribbons can be removed and burnt or buried after a period or may be left on the tree.

Herbs

Herbs are plants used for food, flavouring, perfume, medicine, and spiritual purposes. Herbs were the main source of medicine for our ancestors, but there was a decline in knowledge and use of healing plants. The word *herb* usually refers to green leafy plant parts, and *spice* to a dried product of seeds, berries, bark, root, or fruits. Herbs can be plants like lavender, shrubs like rosemary, or tress like bay laurel. Some plants like coriander are used as both herbs and spices. Some herbs like mint are used for both culinary and medicinal purposes.

Herbs stimulate elimination of toxins from the body, cleanse, and can be used to smudge or create sacred space. Herbs are used internally as infusions (teas), decoctions (boiled to extract oils), tinctures (material extracted in alcohol), syrups, or essences. They are used externally in baths, ointments, compresses, poultices, infused oils, essential oils, fragrances, and incense.

Herbs have long been used in traditional medicine and pharmaceuticals originated in herb medicine, with some drugs still being extracted from plants. As well as healing, we use herbs for divination, contacting spirits, cleansing, and protection. Various herbs can also be used to help induce vivid or lucid dreaming or dream recall.

Key Ritual: Journey to Retrieve a Power Plant for Yourself

The intention is to journey to retrieve a power plant yourself or to ask one of your helping spirits to do a power plant retrieval for you.

Lucie

I got a lotus flower. It was white and in the center pink. I think it is to do with wisdom, for me to see things differently, like lotus flowers are beautiful on top but the roots are in the mud, and it is an ever-changing relationship between what you see and what you feel. Whatever is mud can be changed to beautiful flowers. I think it is mainly wisdom and mainly patience as well because it doesn't bloom quickly.

I think it is specifically for me. I didn't just see the flower; I really saw everything in the root. It flew to me weirdly; it flew into me. It was very nice. What was amazing in this journey is that the jaguar came. It is the first time ever I was journeying with the jaguar, so I was happy. His role seems to be mainly to seal things and he sealed the lotus in.

How to Do the Key Ritual

Have the intention to journey to retrieve a power plant that wants to work with you. Retrieve only one plant in this journey. You are not usually journeying with an intention to retrieve a specific plant unless you feel strongly this is a plant you are to work with, and spirit confirms this during the journey. Journey to a location you are guided to go to.

A power plant or other helping spirit should be waiting for you. If one is not waiting for you, then search until you find one. Confirm that a spirit is your power plant or a helping spirit.

If you meet a spirit who will perform the power plant retrieval, they may have the power plant with them or may ask you to wait and go to find it for you. They will then put the power plant in one of your chakras, usually the heart chakra. The spirit may place the plant in you, blow it into you, or invite the plant to run, fly or dive into your energy body. They may then seal it in you. Return to physical reality bringing the power plant with you.

The other method is to meet the power plant and invite it to merge with you in spiritual reality and return with it. The plant may enter a chakra or simply merge with you. If it does not you can pull the spirit into your body. Return to physical reality with the power plant as above.

Accept the plant unless you are guided strongly that you do not want to work with the plant for some reason, which should not be the case.

You can subsequently journey to the power plant to ask how you will work with it.

Other Rituals

Other rituals that you can perform include: journey to meet a plant guardian spirit, journey to retrieve a power plant for another person, journey to get a crop ritual, journey to a poisonous plant, and journey to perform plant psychopomp.

Journey to Meet a Plant Guardian Spirit

The intention is to journey to a spirit that look after plants, to find out about them and get permission to work with plants or any other advice that the spirit has for us.

Lilian

> It did not show me a face but energy. It looks like water
> vapour above the plants. It said we are like the beekeep-
> ers, tending to all the plants. It said we are all together, all
> one, the trees, mosses and ferns. Unlike the animal and
> mineral kingdoms, the plant kingdom is tightly knit. They
> said plants were the original healers, and plants contain
> solutions to all the illnesses we have. It is like a web that
> connects them all.

Journey to Retrieve a Power Plant for Another Person

The intention is to journey to retrieve a power plant that wants to work with
a person, or can be more specific, such as to find a power plant that wants to
work with the person to address a particular issue they are experiencing in
their lives. You may lie beside the person during the journey. The person for
who the plant is being retrieved does not journey.

Look for a plant and waits to see several perspectives or representations
of it to confirm it is the person's plant. This usually involves seeing different
sides of the plant. When a power plant has been found clutch it to your chest
in spiritual reality or place it in your heart chakra, or a tool like a crystal, and
return with it to physical reality. The energy of the power plant is then blown
into the person's heart and crown chakras. You can scoop energy out of your
heart chakra with your hands and blow the energy into them through your
hands. Seal the power plant in by rattling over the two chakras as guided.

Tell the person what plant has been retrieved and explain to them how
to work with it. You might want to advise the person to conduct their own
research into the meaning a power plant has for them, rather than read a
description of this from a book.

Lucie

> It is ivy. It came very quickly. I was not sure it was the
> plant as it was everywhere and I started exploring other
> things, but it came after me! I thought Okay, maybe I am
> not looking for the plant, but the plant is looking for me.
> I asked what it was for and I saw you with clothes made of
> ivy. It looked really beautiful. It looks like protection but

then there was a voice telling me it was also how plants communicate, there is a network effect. When you want to work with nature you can use it for that.

I saw the spirit of the plant. I didn't see that for my own power plant. It looked pretty much like you. Also, there were bees attached to the ivy. I saw that when I was a kid and my house had ivy with bees. So, you have ivy and bees.

Journey to Get a Crop Ritual

The intention is to journey to retrieve rituals that can be used in a ceremony dedicated to ensuring a fertile and abundant crop. If you are not working on the land this is an indirect way of working with crops. The intention here is to journey to the spirit of rice to ask for a ritual. Replace this with another crop if this is more relevant for you. This can be subsequently performed in a ceremony in nature. This may be done as an individual or group ritual, with individual journey input being used to design a composite ceremony with different rituals.

Lilian

I journeyed to the rice fields and saw a toad which I assumed was the rice spirit. It brought me somewhere very hot and said to capture the energy of the sun. I couldn't figure this out and it said you could start a fire with a magnifying glass. I have never done that and said can I use a lighter or match instead; it said it is not ideal, but I can.

It said to put a large bowl and start a fire inside it to capture the sun energy at noon when the sun is highest. Start a fire and pulverise uncooked rice, put it in alcohol and put it into the fire. Let it burn to ashes, then put water over it and release this water into a stream, which releases the spirit, so that it can go off to the fields. This also helps sustain and increase subsequent cycles.

Journey to a Poisonous Plant

The intention is to journey to the spirit of a poisonous plant to find out about them.

Lilian

It said a lot of these plants are very old and we are not compatible with them, although there could be points in our evolution when we can use them. What is poisonous to us is not always to other plants or animals. They sometimes also need to be poisonous to recover.

Journey to Perform Plant Psychopomp

The intention is to psychopomp plant spirits.

Sam

I asked the souls here to listen and if they wanted help to ask. Some of the souls listened to me and I handled one that was very confused and was half plant and half human with branches around her. I sat her down, combed her hair and she became more of a lady. I explained to her that she was not in a body anymore and my angel took her to the light.

Pro Tips

The following tips are provided:

1. **Sustainability.** Be careful not to over-harvest the plants in a local area. When working with plants avoid killing plants or insects that are part of its environment.

2. **Comfort.** When working with plants in nature bring things that make it comfortable for you to sit with a plant like a blanket or mosquito net.

3. **Patience.** Effects of working with plants may be incremental and take time to manifest. It is important to be patient and not expect quick results.

4. **Poisonous plants.** Some plants are poisonous or harmful to skin. Some essential oils are toxic. Do not use a plant part or product unless you are sure that it is safe to use.

5. **Contraindications.** Be aware of what plant material is not suitable for use with children, pregnant women, nursing mothers, or animals.

Also make sure that a plant does not have contraindications for any medicine being taken before using it.

MINERALS

The mineral kingdom includes rocks (aggregates), crystals/gems (minerals/ rocks), and metals (rock extracts). There are individual mineral spirits, spirits that represent mineral types, and spirits that look after minerals in general. Ways you can work with minerals include:

1. Power mineral retrieval

2. Mineral communication and healing

3. Working with rocks

4. Working with crystals

5. Working with metals

6. Working with blacksmiths

Shamans may make medicine bundles or bags that contain rocks, crystals, and other power objects found in nature. These are usually made with animal skin or cloth and are used in rituals, typically by the practitioner or a person selecting one of more of the bundle contents to be used in divination or healing.

Mineral Communication and Healing

You can use the same basic approach for communicating with animals to communicate with minerals. This may be direct or via an intermediary spirit. If a mineral does not appear to communicate or work with you, hold it and you should feel some sort of shift in your body as it attunes to the mineral.

There are many methods to use crystals in healing. They can be placed near or on a person who needs healing or used to clear a person, balance energy in them, or amplify power directed at them. Clear crystals after each use. Commonly used approaches for healing are:

1. Using a crystal to scan the body of a person to find areas of imbalance or where healing is needed. The crystal can be used to clear energy by passing it over the area or placing the non-terminator (round) end

of the crystal on the area and intending that energy is released, or to direct energy into the area using the terminator (pointed) end.

2. Placing crystals on the chakras with the intention of clearing and balancing them.

3. Putting a crystal on a location where there is pain and rotating the crystal in a clockwise direction to draw out the discomfort or leaving it for a while to absorb the discomfort and then removing and clearing the crystal.

4. Using a crystal in extraction healing to collect energy which is transformed or released from the crystal by placing it in water or earth or passing it through incense or a flame. A rattle holding crystals can also be shaken over a person to extract intrusions.

5. Using a crystal as a receptacle to hold energy retrieved in power animal retrieval, soul retrieval or destiny retrieval.

Power Mineral Retrieval

You work with power minerals, spirits who may be rocks, crystals, gemstones, or metals. Preparatory work may be done with a mineral helper prior to journeying to meet it. This can involve holding it, carrying it, meditating with it, or dieting with it to connect to and establish a relationship with the mineral. A journey can be taken to find and meet the mineral spirit, which may look different from the physical mineral.

A power mineral is retrieved by you or for another person in the same way as a power animal. If a power mineral is retrieved, you can journey with the power mineral or use it in rituals.

Rocks

Rocks are used as tools and altars, worshipped, in ritual, and can be portals to other realms. Mountains are regarded as the home of deities, with sacred rocks often located at their top or base. In Japan, rocks are the spiritual heart of shrines and the bodies of kami (spirits). In Mongolia, ovoos are rock cairns that are sites of spirit worship. Standing stones may be hunting grounds, calendars, ceremonial sites, burial grounds, or spirit homes. Art is carved in rocks (petroglyphs) or painted on rocks (pictographs), and often contains shamanic symbols.

Some rock rituals are initiatory, including rock polishing and rock grinding. In rock polishing two buckets are used, one filled with rocks. Rocks are taken out of the bucket one at a time, polished with a cloth, and placed in the other bucket. After a while, a consciousness shift occurs. In rock grinding a small and large rock are ground together with the intention of communicating with spirit. You go to a place in nature, find a large stone with a flat surface and a smaller stone, and grind them together. A rock spirit may then communicate with you.

Crystals

Crystals are power objects. Shamans consider crystals to be living entities that interact with us and bridge spiritual and physical reality. They are used for divination, seeing into the past, present, or future, or other realms, and in healing modalities such as extraction. Healing crystals were traditionally passed on to successors. In journeys, crystals are sometimes inserted into a person's energy body by spirits; such journeys are initiatory in nature.

Some crystals possess an electrical charge known as piezoelectricity that is emitted from crystals if they are pressed. Crystals have their own vibrational frequencies, which allows us to use energies specific to each crystal.

Crystals are used to collect, hold, transmute, amplify, direct and focus energy. The terminator of a crystal (the pointed end) indicates the direction of energy flow. They can be programmed with intentions, used to amplify power or raise your vibration, open chakras, and help to develop psychic abilities. Crystals can be carried, worn or put in an area, and used for healing, clearing space, protection, empowerment, divination, focusing energy, or on altars and shrines. As well as being tools, they are also used to construct other tools such as wands.

When choosing a crystal to work with you can read about them but should also visit an ethical crystal seller to see which ones you feel attracted to or that call to you, allowing your intuition to select types of crystal and individual crystals to work with. Confirm that it wants to work with you by asking it to communicate this to you. Try to find out from where and how stones are sourced. One way to work with crystals regularly is to wear them as jewellery. When crystals are to be used in healing, it is important to know their polarity, which way the energy flows inside them. With cut and polished crystals, their polarity may be altered.

Crystals are cleared by setting an intention and visualizing energy leaving the crystal as you put it in running water, salt water, salt, earth, sunlight, moonlight, smudge it or pass it through a flame. However, be careful not to place soluble crystals in water or to use salt water on ones that can be damaged by this. Crystals can also be cleared with sound, by merging with a helping spirit while holding a crystal, or with selenite which can be used to clear other crystals. Crystals should be cleared before and after use.

Crystals can be charged by exposing them to the sun or moon. You can also merge with a helping spirit and ask it to empower a crystal you are holding. After you acquire or are gifted a crystal you should sit with it in meditation or journey to it to establish a connection with it and receive communication about how you can work with it.

You can work with a crystal with known properties or program a crystal to attract and amplify energies relevant to how you want it to work with you, by holding the crystal and focusing on the specific energy you wish to program it with. Working with a crystal synchronises your energy with it. Work with one crystal at a time so you know what its messages are. Meditate with them, ask to meet them in dream or journey to a crystal to ask how it should be used and how to develop and deepen our relationship with it.

The crystal most used by shamans is clear crystal quartz, which is regarded as a master crystal. Quartz crystals can guide and protect a shaman in a journey. We can see from excavations at ancient burial sites that our ancestors used quartz crystals and buried them with the dead.

Each type of crystal has many correspondences and associations. The crystals that shamanic practitioners commonly work with, and their main uses, are:

1. **Amethyst.** Used to calm and enhance psychic abilities (especially intuition).

2. **Celestobarite.** A combination of celestite and barite energies used in shamanic journeying (especially to the middle world), and exploring the past, present and future.

3. **Jade.** Used to attract luck and prosperity, protect against illness, and for dream work.

4. **Jasper.** Associated with shamans and priests. Used to ground and for farsightedness.

5. **Labradorite.** Used for transformation, aura protection, chakra balancing, finding your purpose, dispelling illusion, and developing psychic and magical abilities.

6. **Lodolite.** Also known as shaman quartz or shamanic dream crystals. This is a quartz variety with inclusions that facilitates internal work, spirit connection, shamanic journeying, past life work, and manifestation. It is also used in dream work.

7. **Menalite.** Associated with rebirth, reincarnation, and coming to terms with death. Is supports shamanic journeying and is used in female rites of passage.

8. **Merlinite.** Used to work with spiritual and earthly energies and to support shamanic rituals, especially for past and future life work.

9. **Nuummite.** Used for grounding, restoring power, insight, past life work, removing blocks, connecting to your authentic self, and shamanic journeying and soul retrieval.

10. **Quartz.** Clear quartz is the shamanic all-purpose crystal. Rose quartz is associated with unconditional love and thus the heart chakra, but can be used to balance all chakras, as well as to promote forgiveness and acceptance of others. Smoky quartz is good for grounding and giving protection during shamanic journeying.

11. **Selenite.** Used in healing, third eye activation, and to clear other crystals.

12. **Tourmaline.** Used for grounding (especially black tourmaline), confidence, and balance.

Another crystal often mentioned in a shamanic context is shamanic star stones (also known as shaman stones or Moqui marbles). These come in male/female pairs and comprise a hematite shell around a sandstone core. They are used to ground, balance energy, activate the third eye, and to promote clairvoyance and visions. However, these stones are only found on National Park Lands in Arizona and Utah and their collection is prohibited.

Metals

A metal is an element, compound, or alloy. An alloy is a mix of two or more elements in which the main component is a metal. Pure metals are often too soft, brittle, or reactive to be used alone; using them in alloys modifies their properties so they can be used. Examples of alloys are bronze (copper and tin) and brass (copper and zinc).

Blacksmiths

There is a long association of blacksmiths with shamanism across cultures and use of metal on shaman's costumes. Blacksmiths may be shamans and are often thought to have hidden knowledge. Blacksmiths were believed to be taught their art by spirits, and then to have handed their skills down, with the role of blacksmith being hereditary. Blacksmiths are regarded as having the patronage and protection of a deity responsible for blacksmithery. Blacksmiths make metal articles for a shaman's costumes and drums and ritual tools. A blacksmith works with iron, a whitesmith with precious metals, and a redsmith with copper.

Key Ritual: Journey to the Mother Crystal

The intention is to ask a power animal or helping spirit to take you to the Mother Crystal.

Lilian

I went upward forever. I was going up an icy crystal mountain and passed through dense fog of some kind. At the top there was a little window, and I went into the mountain. The Mother Crystal appeared. She was enormous with arms like wings, Egyptian like. She spoke to me about how her core was with Mother Earth, but she resides in this separate universe.

I merged with and disintegrated into her. There was a feeling of weightlessness. It was surreal. She spoke to me about ancient civilisations which knew how to work with crystals, realigning on a molecular level.

They had a master crystal ball that could charge other crystals for healing. They were aligned with the stars and light. They could be laser-like in terms of their ability to address a problem, like surgery of some kind. I also got some advice about my life. It was hard for me to disengage from her.

How to Do the Key Ritual

You may take a journey with one or more of the following intentions:

1. To meet the Mother Crystal and to ask her how you should work with crystals in general.

2. To journey to her and ask to get information about how to work with one or more physical crystals. You do this by holding them in turn on your chest with one hand on top of the crystal and asking how they should be prepared, used, and cleared, or how they can be used for a specific use such as divination or healing.

3. Asking for permission to merge with the Mother Crystal to experience her power. You may also receive a teaching or healing from her, and such journeys can be initiatory.

4. You might want to take an offering that you are guided is suitable for her.

The above journeys can be taken as individual journeys or as a collective journey. If you are new to shamanic work, it may be best to perform them individually. If you merge with the Mother Crystal, remember to unmerge from her before you return to physical reality.

Other Rituals

Other rituals that you can perform include: journey to meet a mineral guardian spirit, journey to retrieve a power mineral for yourself, journey to retrieve a power mineral for another person, journey to the spirit of a crystal, journey to the Blacksmith, and journey to perform mineral psychopomp.

Journey to Meet a Mineral Guardian Spirit

The intention is to journey to a guardian spirit that looks after minerals to find out about them and get permission to work with minerals, or other advice the spirit has for us.

>*Ann*
>
>I met the spirit who was rather tall and floaty looking. I asked what their role was and was given a description of the earth. They described the plant kingdom as being like a cloak put around the earth, and inside the earth there is a powerful energy in the core and that energy is what we can tap into (which is why they tell us to lie on the earth).
>
>Within that there are the rocks and minerals, which are part of a whole and which all have a different role. I was also told to forget about the book that I look at when I buy crystals. They laughed at me. They said rather than looking up their purpose on the internet or in books take it in my hand and ask it what its function is and do not be so analytical about it.
>
>Their role is to protect the energy inside the earth which we can all use. I was given some advice about some diamonds I possess that I had forgotten about and never wear. These are inherited items, and they will maintain an ancestral connection for me. I should put them in a ring and wear it.

Power Mineral Retrieval for Yourself

The intention is to journey to retrieve a power mineral that wants to work with you. Retrieve only one mineral in this journey. You are not usually journeying with an intention to retrieve a specific mineral unless you feel strongly this is a mineral you are to work with, and spirit confirms this during the journey. Journey to a location you are guided to go to.

A power mineral or other helping spirit should be waiting for you. If one is not waiting for you, then search until you find one. Confirm that a spirit is your power mineral or a helping spirit.

If you meet a spirit who will perform the power mineral retrieval, they may have the power mineral with them or may ask you to wait and go to find it for you. They will then put the power mineral in one of your chakras, usually the heart chakra. The spirit may place the mineral in you, blow it into you, or invite the mineral to run, fly or dive into your energy body. They may then seal it in you. Return to physical reality bringing the power mineral with you.

The other method is to meet the power mineral and invite it to merge with you in spiritual reality and then return with it. The mineral may enter a chakra or simply merge with you. If it does not do this, you can reach out and pull the spirit into your body. Again, return to physical reality with the power mineral as above.

Accept the mineral unless you are guided strongly that you do not want to work with the mineral for some reason, which should not be the case.

You can subsequently journey to the power mineral to ask how you will work with it.

Maya

I asked the eagle if I could be introduced to my mineral and I went into this cave. There was something like malachite. I was like, "So am I working with you?"

There was no response, so maybe not. There were stalactites and I said, "I don't even know if you are a mineral, but am I working with you?"

I heard another voice saying, "You're working with me." It was Iron. It was really cagey though. Like, I was having a hard time tonight.

I said, "So how do I work with you?"

"You'll find out."

"How do I find out?"

"Later."

"Should I Google you?"

"No."

"So how am I supposed to learn about you?"

He was like, "You have to ask the right questions."

Oh gee. I thought, Okay, I'll try again. So then basically we got to the point where I understood the purpose of iron and something about strength, but I still don't know how to use it. He said he would reveal it to me later.

Journey to Retrieve a Power Mineral for Another Person

The intention is to journey to retrieve a power mineral that wants to work with a person, or can be more specific, such as to find a power mineral that wants to work with the person to address a particular issue that they are experiencing in their lives. You may lie beside the person during the journey. For the avoidance of doubt, the person for who the mineral is being retrieved does not journey.

Look for a mineral and waits to see several perspectives or representations of it to confirm it is the person's mineral. This usually involves seeing different sides of the mineral. When a power mineral has been found clutch it to your chest in spiritual reality or place it in your heart chakra, or a tool like a crystal, and return with it to physical reality. The energy of the power mineral is then blown into the person's heart and crown chakras. You can scoop energy out of your heart chakra with your hands and blow the energy into them through your hands. Seal the power mineral in by rattling over the two chakras as guided.

Tell the person what mineral has been retrieved and explain to them how to work with it. You might want to advise the person to conduct their own research into the meaning a power mineral has for them, rather than read a description of this from a book.

Sophia

Her power mineral is a jagged piece of obsidian, black obsidian. It came very quickly. It was right there straight away. I knew which piece to bring as it seemed that the master mineral was there, and they gave me a little piece of it. I got some advice about how to use it. Different edges or sides can give you different insights, things to look into. It is grounding and healing.

Journey to the Spirit of a Crystal

In this journey you can hold a crystal that you want to work with and have the intention to journey to its spirit to communicate with it and find out how to work with it or any other advice that it has for you. Let the crystal transport you. Ask how you should work with it. Be aware of vibrations, feelings, sensations and insights. When you return, disconnect from the crystal and ground.

Lilian

The moment I held it I felt that it was a friend; there was a familiar energy to it. It said talk to me like you would to a friend. It said I will find joy and taught me to connect with my dreams.

Journey to the Blacksmith

The intention is to journey to the archetypal spirit known as the Blacksmith to understand their role and to learn how we might use metals for healing. We can ask them for a healing.

James

I journeyed up and saw a typical blacksmith and a horse together. They said that relationship was strong and can be very spiritual. If a blacksmith was aware of the spirits and respected them while he was working, the relationship can be very positive.

The blacksmith put a brand on me and horseshoes to my hands and feet and nailed them in. There was a priest with the blacksmith and horse and it was like a marriage. They said you can be part of this if you want, and I said yes.

He made bracelets for me and taught me about fire and water and what metal can be used for. He said there was a strong link between me and the horse, put chains between me and the horse, and said if I want to accept the chains, we can create this relationship. He said the chains could be seen as negative, but they symbolised a strong connection. I accepted them.

Journey to Perform Mineral Psychopomp

The intention is to psychopomp mineral spirits.

> *Ann*
>
>> I got a helping spirit who was large and translucent. I was told to come this way quickly. I followed and we walked until we came to a rose quartz crystal. I was told to pick it up. I did so and it pulsated with light and I felt a lot of power. I was told to take it to the Sacred Garden. When I got to this beautiful garden in the lower world, I was told to let go of it. It flew into the air, sparkled and disappeared into rays of light.

Pro Tips

The following tips are provided:

1. **Buying crystals.** Only buy crystals from ethical dealers.

2. **Crystal energy.** Ensure a crystal matches your own vibration and intended purpose.

3. **Approach.** Mineral should be approached and used with respect, recognising their power and gifts. Establish a relationship and talk to them as you would to a friend.

4. **Fractured crystals.** Crystals may fracture over time. This does not mean that they are being wrongly used or cannot continue to be used effectively.

5. **Poisonous minerals.** Some minerals and metals are toxic or can harm the skin. Do not use any mineral or mineral product, such as an elixir, unless you are sure it is safe.

ELEMENTAL SPIRITS

Elemental spirits are made of and move through an element that they are associated with, and have power over, and are often invisible. In the Western tradition there are four elemental categories: air, fire, water, and earth elementals. They are sometimes referred to as nature spirits, but nature spirits include other types of spirits.

Air elementals are referred to by the general name *sylphs*, fire elementals by the general name *salamanders*, water elementals by the general name *undines* (although other types include nymphs, sprites, and merfolk), and earth elementals by the general name *gnomes* (although other types include elves, dwarves, and brownies).

Elementals can live longer than humans and dissolve into their element at death. Sometimes they are believed not to have souls and to be incapable of spiritual development, but most of them are highly moral. Some elementals resemble humans, may have homes and jobs, and join in community events. They sometimes fight one another or use the element they are associated with against the element of another elemental.

Elementals can enter relationships with humans. If an elemental weds a mortal, the mortal becomes immortal, and if an elemental weds an immortal the immortal becomes mortal. Immaculate conception is sometimes thought to represent the union of a human with an elemental. Elementals often appear in mythology, legends, and fairy tales.

Air Elementals

Air elementals influence weather conditions. They have keen senses, live on mountain tops or in wind or cloud, have the highest vibrational rate of elementals, and can live for centuries. They are often invisible but can assume human form and communicate with us. Muses were believed to be sylphs, attracted to and inspiring artists. Air elementals are mirthful and eccentric; geniuses often display sylph-like behavior due to their association with these spirits.

Fire Elementals

Fire elementals are the most powerful of the elementals, and we cannot easily communicate with them. They may be sensed in flames or smoke from incense or visible as small balls of light or tongues or fire or seen in lizard-like shapes. They can create fire but can be dangerous. They influence all beings with a fiery temperament. Being in their presence may boost your will and power but may produce negative emotions if you have repressed anger.

Water Elementals

Water elementals work with vital essences and liquids, being present in everything containing water. They are often attractive and symbolized as female and are friendly to humans. They inhabit fountains, waterfalls, rivers, and seas. They are emotional, empathic, and perceptive, and often have visionary and psychic abilities. Mermaids are the best-known Water elementals. There are many legends about these spirits associating with human fishermen.

Earth Elementals

Earth elementals are often smaller than us. Some live in caves, work with stones, gems, and metals, and are supposed to guard treasure buried in the earth. They may be tree or forest guardians or associated with individual plants. They are friendly to humans and can heal broken bones. They may be melancholy or compulsive, or miserly, but can also be nurturing. They are fond of eating and engage in harvest rituals. They often fix or transform things.

Key Ritual: Journey to Meet a Water Elemental Spirit

The intention is to journey to meet a water elemental spirit to understand their nature, and ask them for wisdom, divination or healing.

> ### *Lucie*
>
> I fly with the Raven to the sea, and there is a huge wave forming in front of us. There is a spirit coming out from the foam of the wave. She tells me she has been talking to me for very long time. Every time I feel sad or I want to understand something I usually go and look at the sea. It is soothing in some way. She tells me it reflects the conversation I have with myself. She is trying to facilitate that. She brings me to a past life. In that life I used to look at the sea and she said, "I was there for you too."
>
> "Okay, since you were there, what happened?"
>
> "Your parents left you because they wanted to find a new place where their life would be better, so they went onboard a ship to find a better land. They left you behind because they had the feeling that it could go wrong, and

that you would have better chances of being adopted by someone."

"Okay, what happened?"

"They died, the trip went wrong, they were right to leave you behind. They didn't leave you behind because they didn't love you, but because they loved you most. You had better chances of surviving by yourself." It is like what happened in this life.

Then all of a sudden after that I am scuba diving but without the equipment and I am following a turtle. I have always been afraid of turtles. Usually when I am diving, I follow them, but once they turn back and follow me, I am scared. She said, "Why do you think you are scared of turtles?"

"I am scared of them because they look like old people and have a judgmental look."

"Don't you think that you are the one having that look? The look is a reflection of you. Don't you think you are a much older soul than the turtle is? It is only a reflection of yourself. Maybe other people look at you like you are the turtle."

After that I come back to the rocks and she gives us two crystals. One is for the Raven, a transparent crystal, like clear quartz. Mine is blue and is beautiful, like a giant sapphire. The last image is of an underwater city. She said, "You will need to go there the next time you come back." The next step is this city; there is something to find out.

How to Do the Key Ritual

In the Arthurian legends, we see female water spirits such as the Lady of the Lake. It is probable that you will meet such a spirit on or near water. You will usually take such a journey using an intention related to an association that water has. This could be a journey to work with emotions, sleep or dreams, or psychic abilities, and your development of such abilities.

Other Rituals

Other rituals that you can perform include: journey to an air elemental spirit, journey to an earth elemental spirit, journey to a fire elemental spirit, and journey to the Mermaid Queen.

Journey to Meet an Air Elemental Spirit

The intention is to journey to meet an air elemental spirit to understand their nature.

Maya

It was not like anything I'd ever experienced before because normally like I talk to the spirits, but this time it was like all images. The spirit was beautiful. It was like a beautiful woman with a fairy-like quality. She was almost see-through and was just so gorgeous. She had long hair and was all floaty, it was literally air, all flowing. So, I introduced myself and said, "What would you like to tell me about creativity?"

The first thing I saw was a human heart, then the same heart with thorns in it. What I understood it was telling me is that creativity takes passion and sometimes you have to re-find that passion. I assume that was the right answer because then it moved to the second image. We went to a volcano and flew into it, burned, came out, healed, flew into the volcano, burned, came out, healed, and it was this trial and tribulation. I understood that you fail, try again, fail and try again, and from each failure you are learning more. You are healing, and through that healing process gaining more insight.

Then we flew into and merged with a tree. The tree went through snapshots, really quickly, of the different seasons, like full of fruit, leaves falling, beautiful, and then covered with snow, coming back. It was its life cycle. Then we were blown over by the wind, some kind of hurricane, and in the death, there was obviously going to be new life. I took this as a metaphor for the cycle of creativity. Even outside forces will come and destroy what you create, but from that new life will spring.

I asked if there was anything else that they wanted to tell me and they were like "Nope, we're done." They just kind of like shooed me. This is like my writing, which I feel is getting better, but sometimes lose passion for, and have to find ways to bring it back. Sometimes you get stuck with the story and it is like the winter period of the tree. Eventually a new idea, like the spring, will dawn. The death part is the end of the book and then something new will come. There will be other trees and other books, and other creative forces to bring in.

Journey to Meet an Earth Elemental Spirit

The intention is to journey to meet an earth elemental spirit to understand their nature. The journey described was to meet the spirit of a super volcano.

Sue

I went in a cave and saw a face in the rock. I introduced myself, its eyes opened, and I started to see a dragon. When I recognized it as a dragon, it came alive. The body was mountains that started to move as it swirled around. I asked how to work with it. The feeling was being at peace and connected with the ancient. There were two things to do: ground myself and join with the volcano energies. I saw lots of roots growing out from me in all directions merging with the rock, silent, at peace. It felt really nice.

Journey to Meet a Fire Elemental Spirit

The intention it to journey to meet a fire elemental spirit to understand their nature.

Sam

I go very deep in the underworld. There is a river of lava, a volcano, and a firebird. There is a fire spirit trapped; they don't let it go because it is out of control. The bird tells me to teach the fire spirit with love, not control. I talk with the fire spirit. It says it will try to stay under control and they agree to release it. The spirit is let out and everything is under control. It gave me a yellow and orange crystal of fire to bring back.

Journey to the Mermaid Queen

The intention is to journey to the Mermaid Queen, who works with all the waters of the earth and also with the moon.

Ludivine

It was nice with a big full moon. I was on a boat and there were a lot of stars in the sky, it was just beautiful. The stars were reflecting on the water so you couldn't see the difference between the sky and the water, and I couldn't see the horizon.

The Mermaid Queen jumped on the boat and I gave her some flowers as an offering. I combed her hair as well. I think I like to comb hair because this is the second time I have done this. She is the queen so she should look nice.

I asked what gift she had. She said, "Open your eyes and see like a child all the wonders of the world. Be amazed by the wonders of the world. Everything is one, you cannot see the horizon, everything is one, there is no separation between anything."

Pro Tips

The following tips are provided:

1. **Respect.** Elemental spirits are powerful, unpredictable, difficult to control, and should be treated with respect.

2. **Right relationship.** You should not betray the trust of or deceive an elemental, or ask them to help with selfish intentions, as they may turn on you.

3. **Directional correspondences.** Remember that in some cultures the correspondence between elements (and therefore elemental spirits) and directions is different.

4. **Creativity.** One way of enhancing creativity is to work with air elementals.

5. **Fire elementals.** Fire elementals are difficult to work with, and it is best not to work with them until you are experienced and comfortable working with this type of spirit.

FAIRIES

The word *fairy* describes a being seen in myth, legend, and folklore, and the word *fae* describes fairy qualities. Fairies, seen in all cultures, are supernatural beings with magical abilities, associated with nature, who can take human form. Fairies tend to avoid humans due to our abuse of nature and demonization of them by religion, but it is possible to work with them.

The Nature of Fairies

There are many theories and beliefs about the origin and nature of fairies. They are variously thought to be deities, nature spirits, ancestral spirits, fallen angels, demons, supernatural beings, elementals, or hidden conquered people. Fairies have some common characteristics:

- **Size.** Fairies, often thought of as small, but are variously sized and can change size.

- **Appearance.** They can be human like but change into other forms like animals. They can appear and disappear, using tools like a magic cap or cloak to become invisible.

- **Attitude to humans.** Some live close to humans and are helpful; others are hostile and ruin crops or steal things if they feel mistreated.

- **Behavior.** They can be solitary or live in groups (troops). They play practical jokes, like hiding items or confusing travelers, and may use trickery and illusion like making "fairy gold" from worthless items. Fairies are believed not to be able to lie.

- **Likes and dislikes.** Fairies like dancing, music, singing, revelry and festivals. They value virtue, kindness, and cleanliness. They dislike greed, untidiness and dirtiness.

- **Nature.** Fairies live in nature and are often viewed as animal guardians. Fairy cows and bulls are reputed to make herds flourish. Fairies are associated with birds like the eagle and owl, and with tress like Rowan that is considered sacred to fairies.

- **Occupations.** Fairies have occupations like hunting, herding, and farming, as well as being smiths, shoemakers, weavers, and spinners.

Fairies live in *fairyland*, in hills, underground, underwater, in forests and sacred groves, by running water, in waterfalls or in caves. They may live in fairy palaces or forts. The entrance to fairyland is often via a pit, pothole, cave, well, knoll, crevice, or hilltop. There is often a relationship between fairies and the dead.

Some humans visit fairyland, where time passes more slowly (one way being by stepping into a fairy ring). Humans who visit fairyland may gain occult knowledge or gifts and become a *Fairy Doctor* able to heal. On returning to the human realm, people often perceive there to have been a long passage of time.

Fairy Myths and Legends

Fairies feature in Celtic and other myths. The Seelie Court contains benevolent fairies, the Unseelie Court malevolent ones. There is also an association between fairies and Arthurian legend. The name of Arthur's stepsister, Morgan le Fay, indicates her fairy nature.

There is folklore about abduction by fairies, often of mortal midwives to help with the birth of fairy children or lactating human mothers to nurse fairy children. Babies can also be abducted by fairies, sometimes with a fairy child, a *changeling*, being substituted for a baby.

It is possible to have a fairy partner and fairies may seduce mortal men and women. The general pattern of such relationships is that a human is attracted to a fairy that consents to a relationship on a certain condition. The human typically breaks this, losing the fairy partner and suffering bad luck, and attempts to renew the relationship, usually with limited success. Fairy partners can provide humans with occult knowledge and magical healing powers.

Protective charms traditionally associated with fairies include iron, church bells, St. John's Wort, or wearing your clothes inside out.

Fairy Work Benefits

There are a number of benefits of working with the fairy realm. These include enhanced imagination and creativity, knowledge and wisdom, attracting good fortune, improved crop harvests and healthy animal herds, being more aligned with nature, improved capabilities in dream work, and companionship.

Working with Fairies

It is possible to see fairies, or otherwise sense their presence, children being particularly sensitive to them. To see them set a strong intention to do so. If you are ready to see fairies, they are aware of this and it encourages them to allow you to see them. Things that help are being innocent, childlike, playful, joyful, having a sense of wonder, and having strong ethics. You are also more likely to see them if you are in nature. Things that are not helpful are not being joyful, being too serious, or being too loud in their presence.

Certain times of the year and day are good for working with fairies such as: quarter and cross-quarter days, full moons, night (especially before midnight), and at dawn and dusk (the times between day and night). Fairies are reputed to disappear at the crow of a cock or at sunrise.

The boundary between our world and the fairy realm is believed to be particularly thin at natural places like rivers, trees, lakes, and hills. Some places used by fairies should though be avoided, like fairy mounds and the fairy paths between them, and fairy rings.

Benevolent fairies like humans and will help you if you give them gifts. You should introduce yourself and establish harmony with fairies that live close to you. You win their confidence by your thoughts and actions. Traditional fairy offerings include sweets and cakes, honey, fruit and vegetables, fruit juices, bread, barley, milk and dairy products like butter and cheese, beer (made from fermented barley), wine and spirits, teas, and spices such as ginger, bay, thyme, rosemary, cinnamon, and basil. You can also make offerings by planting something in nature or giving animals affection.

Fairies are particularly helpful in creative work. If you want to involve fairies in creative work, set an intention related to this. This will attract fairies who want to help and who are interested in acting in the capacity of a muse.

Fairies were often associated with agricultural gods and goddesses and crop and milk yields, which led to their being made regular offerings. Often the first and last portion of a fruit or vegetable harvest was offered to them.

Key Ritual: Journey to the Fairy Queen

The intention is to journey to meet the Fairy Queen to introduce yourself, pay your respects to her, and ask permission to work with the fairy realm.

James

I went down to a strange world that was a bit mixed, not exactly the lower world but had some elements of it. I saw the Fairy Queen. She was wearing a black and silver costume. I knelt and gave her a cake with cinnamon on. She liked it. After a while I said, "Can I get up?" and she said yes. She put her hands in a ball and produce something. She said it was a fairy lamp.

I followed her to a stable where I was shown the relationship between the fairies and horses and told it would be good for me to work with horses. I asked about the horses in the stables, they were not wild. They indicated the horses do not mind their environment; it is a comfortable relationship for them.

I became aware of another figure. He came around and tried to steal the lamp from me. I said it was a gift and he could not just steal it. The Fairy Queen smiled and said fairies have a bit of an edge to them and you have to be aware of it.

They showed me that I could work with horses in the fairy world, including healing their bodies, birthing, and things like that. I was given an indication that as I was more earthy than they are it helps, and vice versa. The guy appeared again, and I gave him a cake. He whispered something in my ear. I feel at the right time I will know what this is.

How to Do the Key Ritual

Have the intention to meet the Fairy Queen. You should take a gift for her, selected from the offerings suggested above. When you arrive in her presence introduce yourself, show her respect, and thank her for letting you be in her presence. Make your offering to her and explain that you would like to learn from her how to work with fairies. She may well give you some general advice in relation to this, and you may also receive other guidance from her. When you have finished thank her for allowing you to meet her and for any advice received.

Other Rituals

Other rituals that you can perform include: journey to meet a fairy helping spirit, journey to the Cauldron of Inspiration and Rebirth, and journey to ask for a fairy healing modality that we can use.

Journey to Meet a Fairy Helping Spirit

The intention is to journey to meet a fairy helping spirit and learn how to work with them.

James

> I asked what I can do for him and he said he had a sore shoulder. I thought that is what I do all day, and he laughed and said he was joking. He asked me to have a drink with him. My guide said it was okay. The fairy said that they set up a barrier with humans with stories about how eating and drinking in fairyland is dangerous. I drank it but felt nauseous. The fairy said I had to respect their power.

Journey to the Cauldron of Inspiration and Rebirth

The intention is to journey to the Cauldron of Inspiration and Rebirth. Cauldrons are seen in Celtic mythology, including that of the Goddess Cerridwen. These cauldrons have magical properties of inspiration, knowledge, and resurrection.

James

I went to the same door with the lamp and went through to a great big round hole. I went down on a rope to have a look and there was a really big cauldron with thick, green, gooey stuff in it. I went in and was in this thick soup. I swam down and went through a tunnel down and down for a long time.

Then I saw an end of it, but as I was trying to come out it was tangled and sticky. I asked my guide for help, and it came to me to use the movement of a circle going left. I started to do that, and it helped me to untangle. I came to a very deep level in the lower world and was told I was able to access this very deep level.

Then I was pulled up. I saw my aboriginal guides and they put a blanket around me and said, "That was a tough one." They told me I can use the lamp to help when discussing things and working with other people. A horse spirit came down and became a man and said there was a deeper connection between us.

I got the lamp and he sat with me and I put the lamp in the middle. I was told I can put it inside me as well. The nausea in the previous journey was to clear to allow for the lamp to be placed inside me.

Journey to Ask for a Fairy Healing Modality that We Can Use

The intention is to journey to ask a fairy spirit helper for a healing modality that we can use. This may be to use with people, animal, plants, minerals, or spirits.

James

I saw my lamp, went through a door and a dashing fairy guy took me around the horses; it is his job to look after them. He told me about food they like. He said I can work with them by using circular hand movements on them. He gave me a book in a bag. I looked at the book; it was called *The Fairy Book of Horse Magic.*

I am going to go on a course to work with horses. The
fairy said, "This is what you need to prepare for the course,
set the intention to learn and read the book."

I looked at it and it was practical. It said people approach
a horse face-on, which they do not like, it is aggressive for
them. It is better to come at them from the side. If I make
circular motions on them it lets them know I work with
the fairies. He taught me how to whisper in their left ear,
and other tips.

Pro Tips

The following tips are provided:

1. **Avoiding problems.** Problems can arise if fairies feel they have been
   mistreated or a promise has been broken. If given a fairy gift you
   must repay it; if you give a gift one will be given back. Be careful
   not to offend them, keep their secrets, guard their privacy, and keep
   promises. Avoid being conceited, greedy, or boastful. Adopt traits
   that fairies approve of like honesty and graciousness. Respect them,
   plants, animals, and the earth. Be open and generous and use good
   manners.

2. **Iron.** When working with fairies, never carry or wear iron or steel
   objects.

3. **Fairy animals.** Animals that are white or have red ears or eyes are
   usually fairy animals.

4. **Fairy paths.** These connect fairy mounds, where fairies live. Do not
   disturb or block these by building or other activity. Fairy paths can be
   harmful to people and animals.

5. **Unseelie Court.** It is recommended not to work with the Unseelie
   Court.

SPIRITS OF PLACE

The term *spirit of place* described both the essence of a place, as well as a spirit
that inhabits it. Spirits of place can be individual or collective land, elemental,

fairy, ancestral, animal, plant, or mineral spirits. They affect the feeling of a place. They may communicate with people who are able to sense them, often taking the form of a person or animal, and may also appear in journeys, dreams, or visions. Spirits of place often appear in myths and folk tales.

Spirits of place can have global, regional, or local scope. Mother Earth or Gaia has global scope; land spirits that protect large areas such as spirits of mountains, water bodies, and forests can have regional scope (that does not respect human boundaries); and a local spirit can exist in a single landscape feature such as rocks, caves, wells, springs, waterfalls, or trees. These spirits may be permanent or temporary and may or may not be bound to a place. There may be several spirits in a location, or the influence of spirits in neighboring places may overlap.

Two related terms are used: *genius loci* and *sacred site*. Genius loci is a protective spirit of place, often viewed as a guardian animal or small supernatural being. A sacred site is a natural location, or an artificial structure built on a power center, where the quality of energy or presence is recognized as being profoundly positive and healing.

Spirits of place influence humans and other entities in a location, can cause strong feelings and emotions in us, and are affected by us. A place may have energetic imprints of dead people or past events, such as disasters or battles, that affect us. They may be friendly or unfriendly, depending on their attitude to humans and past activities, and may act negatively toward those that cause damage or breach taboos. However, if you develop a relationship with them, they can help make land fertile, protect from accidents, and guard a location.

Spirits of place continue to exist while they are empowered and have a purpose and may remain in the landscape after a feature that they are associated with has disappeared. Their role can change over time because of changes in the location or human activities.

Land Spirits

Land spirits, or *land wights*, are guardian spirits that are strongly tied to a location or natural object, such as a tree or well, and in folklore may be unable to leave that place or object. Land spirits influence us through our emotions and affect the safety and fertility of land.

They may be allies and offer protection, wisdom, and abundance, but are also protective of the land and intolerant of its mistreatment. Some land spirits want to be left alone and do not want to work with people, who they blame for harming land; others are ancestral human spirits who return after death to protect land or look after specific landscape features.

You should honor and be in right relationship with the spirits of the land that you live on or travel through. When people migrate to a new place, some of their ancestral wights come with them and may join or affect the native wights. Land spirits may leave a location.

Sacred Sites

Sacred sites are associated with landscape features, significant to people, and often home to guardian spirits that oversee a site. Sites include natural places like wells, springs, and special trees, with female spirits being associated with borderlands, marshes, water, and caves. They also include constructed sites like stone circles, standing stones, burial chambers, and temples. Structures are often aligned with events such as solstices or equinoxes, or with stars or constellations. They are thus also often associated with festivals to mark agricultural cycles.

A site may mark a myth, legend, or battle, and be associated with rituals like healing, baptism, initiation, rites of passage, and visions. If a sacred site is acknowledged and treated with respect its power increases over time. These places were and are often sites of pilgrimage. People would settle at such sites, and petition sacred site spirits for crop or livestock fertility, good weather, protection, healing, and divination. This often involved dream incubation, where a person fell asleep and a spirit of place would deliver healing or divination in a dream. Sacred sites may be connected forming a larger sacred territory or landscape, usually referred to as *sacred geography*. This involves large scale structures such as ley lines and song lines.

House Spirits

House spirits, also referred to as *house wights*, may be present on the land a property is built on, take up residence when a property is built, or arrive with new residents. House spirits include spirits seen in folklore like brownies, ghosts of people who lived there when alive, or spirits attracted to the place or by activities that occur there. For instance, ritual practices and spirit communication will attract spirits to a property.

Land and house spirits are affected by human actions, thoughts, and words, which have a positive or negative effect on them, leading them to accept or reject the presence of residents in a property. House spirits can be upset by loud noises, disturbances, violent events, or by being ignored. It is advisable to avoid slamming doors, which may be locations spirits live.

House spirits may react to actions that upset them by hiding things, causing machinery to malfunction, or causing accidents, disease and bad luck. However, if a relationship is mutual established between residents and house spirits, they will protect the location, and can offer other benefits including assisting artistic creativity.

Working with Spirits of Place

Do not just assume spirits of place want to work with you but establish relationships with them. Spirits may not want to be in relationship with you, at least initially, but persevere with them. They should eventually befriend you if you approach them respectfully.

Take only what you need from land and make reciprocal exchanges, offering something in return for what you are provided from nature. Walk in nature, acknowledge, respect and make offerings to land spirits, observe cycles and seasons, and understand local practices and traditions. This brings you into relationship with them. For offerings to land and house spirits, use culturally appropriate foods or other items they want to receive.

If a spirit of place is angered, try to find out what caused this and what needs to be done to remedy things. This may involve remedial actions or changing behavior. Spirits may suggest actions like restoring damaged areas, planting, or seed dispersal. Connect with land by walking on it, showing the boundary of the land that you are willing to act as a caretaker for. You may also do work to encourage spirits of place that have left a location to return. In some situations, it may be useful to disengage from a spirit of place that has a negative influence.

Communicate with spirits of place before visiting a location explaining why you are going and what you want to do. Confirm that they have no issues with your intentions. Spirits may deter you from visiting, or lead you away from, specific locations. When entering or leaving land, perform rituals to acknowledge spirits or to say farewell. Such rituals are traditionally referred to as land-taking and land-leaving. Be guided to places that draw you, and open to communicating with spirits there. You may feel that you are being watched in a location or feel that you are welcome in a place, or conversely do not belong there.

Ask for permission to enter a specific site and be open to receiving a message or allow your intuition to guide you. Ask spirits of the land, trees, and plants if they have guidance for you of it there is anything that you can do for them. You may receive communication intuitively or in the form of images or symbols. They might ask for watering or plant maintenance. Ask for permission to perform any rituals. Make offerings and give thanks when you leave.

With house spirits, confirm what they would like you to do. Just clearing residual energies and attract energies you prefer may not be a right approach. Show respect to spirits that live in a property and do not try to remove them. Observe any reasonable restrictions if they ask you to do so. Creating altars or shrines, and performing rituals, tends to get the attention of house spirits, who may then acknowledge you. The best place to work with and make offerings to house spirits is the center of the property, often a location such as a hearth or its equivalent. You can also work with spirits of land and houses in journeys, dreams, or meditation.

Key Ritual: Journey to Gaia

The intention is to journey to meet Gaia.

Ludivine

> I started in space. I saw Earth, but it was quite brief. I went to a desert. It was very yellow and very bright, like a sun. It was very dry with no plants, like an American desert with small red mountains. I knew she was there. She was in a cavern. She was an old lady with a veil or something, very simple. I took her hands and felt like I was a child, and she was healing me. I felt it was just amazing to have this connection.

I felt vibration and current passing and I really like it; it was really nice. At one point we even kissed on the lips. It was beautiful. I said, "Thank you for presenting yourself to me, I am grateful, it is beautiful to see you. How can I help, how can I work with you, what can I do for you?" I was very humble.

I looked around and the landscape became like scenes from all the landscapes of earth. It was full of trees, and jungle, and mountains, everything all in one place. She said that I could place something on my altar to honor her, which would be a good start to work with her. We held hands again and she gave me love.

How to Do the Key Ritual

Journey to meet Gaia with the intention to understand her nature. When you meet her introduce yourself and show respect to her. You may want to make an offering to her, perhaps getting advice from one of your helping spirits about what a suitable offering would be.

The main aim is to understand her, to ask her for a teaching or advice about how you might work with her or the earth, and to ask what else you could do for her. She might offer you healing. You might also ask how you could heal the earth. When you have finished, thank her and return.

Other Rituals

Other rituals that you can perform include: journey to meet a regional spirit of place, journey to meet a local spirit of place, journey to meet a guardian spirit, and journey to perform soul retrieval for a spirit of place.

Journey to Meet a Regional Spirit of Place

The intention is to journey to meet a regional spirit of place to find out about them and how we might help or work with them. Such spirits may be harder to work with than local spirits.

Maya

I went to meet the spirit of the Appalachian Mountains. We were flying over Kentucky. It was like the smoke you see in the mountains. It was just not friendly. I asked what it was doing, and it was kind of monitoring all elements, they said even like the smallest piece of soil has a spirit and they are all connected and intertwined.

The spirit was basically not happy with humans. They didn't care about humans, but they also weren't happy. They sometimes make problems for humans when they do things that they need to rebalance. We had come to a vista on a rock. I said, "Okay, that sucks, is there any way that I can help you?"

They were just kind of like "As if you could do anything."

"You know, I can try."

There was apparently nothing I could do. I said, "What do you see in the future?" and it was terrifying. The images that flashed were from five years from now when there is going to be a huge fire that decimates a large part of the forest, it's horrible, its all gone, unbelievable numbers of species will die because of human activities.

It was kind of prodding me, it was like, "You know what you could do is walk the trail next year, write a book about it and get people on the trail." He was saying that we are in the head too much. He said the Tibetan Buddhists are careful what they step on because they recognise that everything has a spirit and humans used to be like that, native peoples used to be like that.

We have to get back to feeling spirit around us, to be in nature and recognise nature is not an adversary. The only way that's going to happen is if books keep coming out about life-changing journeys. He said some tribes have moved back and some in the north and the Cherokee

lands have the old ways, and they are the only hope. This
is so bleak. I said, "Should I go work with them?"

"No, you leave them alone."

They gave me a place to meet them if I do walk the trail.
They said I need to start at the end of March, start from the
North and walk down to the end and write about it. There
was spot for us to meet and they showed it. Then it was
like, "Bye."

"What if my health isn't good enough?"

"Your body is fine, it's your mind that is not. Your body
resembles your mind, so when your mind is in order and
you are back with spirit, and when everything becomes
what is needs to become, then your body will follow. You
have no problems with your body, it is just your mind."

Journey to Meet a Local Spirit of Place

The intention is to journey to meet a local guardian spirit to find out about
them, if there are issues that concern them, and what you can do to help or
work with them. These spirits may not always be easier than the regional
spirits to work with.

Maya

I went to the main spirit of the river. This spirit was also
not so helpful. It was the same dramatic, "You're killing
the earth."

"Yeah, I get that, but how can I help you?"

"Get rid of humans."

I tried to explain, "I can't get rid of them, what else could
I do?"

The spirit was like, "Just get rid of them."

Then it was like sort of a barter. I was like "All right,
is there any way I can continue." The spirit gave me

permission to build an Eco house and continue to buy land and do the things I want to do. It was happy with my mother because she only plants native flowers to help the pollinators and stuff like that. It said no more than a hundred people a day on the river. Right now, it is up to five hundred and it is too much, and no boats.

I said, "Can we do rescue boats?" and they said okay.

I don't know how that is going to happen. I asked, "Do you have any recommendations about how I do this?"

"Go back and be involved in the government."

I was like, oh my God. I don't want to do that. I understand that is how you change things, and so does the spirit. At first it was only sixty or seventy people a day and I just can't do that. I don't have control of humans. So, I asked, "Is there anything else I could do?"

"No, just get rid of the humans."

Finally, I asked, "Can I come visit you again?"

"No. Don't come back."

Ouch! Then I asked another question, "Can I talk to you again, maybe that was the wrong question?"

"No."

"Can I see you again?"

"Yes, but only when I invite you."

That was the part that was interesting because then the spirit changed a little bit. It was pushing me away and then it said, "Right, one hundred people on the river per day, you can build the house as long as it is an eco house." It showed me the river in ten years which looked awful.

It also said, "You have to go and clean the river every day."

Every day! Oh my God. What about when I go on vacation?

The kayakers are okay though. It is just a problem with the boats. I need to do community awareness about the use of pesticides and talk about planting plants that don't need pesticide would and could help them to see what it might look like if it were more natural. Stuff like that I can do. It's one of the first journeys I've had, which was not great.

Maya has established a working relationship with the spirit and is able to negotiate a workable compromise. Although the journey may seem difficult, a lot of progress has been made.

Journey to Meet a Guardian Spirit

The intention is to meet a guardian spirit of place so you can understand its nature and the effect it has on people and other entities. Ask it how you can work with it.

Sue

I saw a little frog with a crown on. Then I saw a stag. I asked, "How can I work with you?" It ran over a road at a place where there is erosion. It left me there and I said, "What do you want me to do about this?"

The stag said, "Explore and learn." I was shown an ancient forest which had been there. They said it was okay as it was coming back.

I said, "So what's with the frog?"

They said, "Oh, we thought we'd just do that for a bit of fun!"

Journey to Perform Soul Retrieval for a Spirit of Place

The intention is to journey to perform soul retrieval for a spirit of place. You can work in spirit to blow parts back into the spirit, or by some other process.

James

I went to Hokkaido and saw the bear spirit. I said, "You need to have soul retrieval." He was reluctant. Eventually he said okay. I cleared some black stuff around his heart and got an image of a bear cub that had left when people came to Hokkaido. The bear was heartbroken by the loss of the cub. He said when the people came, they had no respect for Ainu traditions.

I grabbed a Shinto priest and put him together with the bear. They started to communicate and identified similarities, and that they could work together. It was the Shinto priest that went to get the spirit and blew it into the Ainu. It symbolised the coming together of cultures.

Pro Tips

The following tips are provided:

1. **Awareness.** Understand spirits of place; if you are not aware of them, you are likely to be motivated unconsciously, or possessed, by them.

2. **Belonging.** We may experience a deep sense of belonging to a place. Spirits that belong to a place sense kinship; you do not feel this at places you do not belong at.

3. **Economic activity.** If we decide the use of a place without reference to spirits of place or local traditions, it can sever ties between spirits and places they reside in.

4. **Constructions.** We should consult spirits of place when building in a location to ensure they agree. We can work with spirits resident in buildings, including homes.

5. **Property rights.** Note that you are caretakers, not owners, of the land. Spirits do not recognize property rights or limits.

CHAPTER 4

INTERMEDIATE WORK

Now that you have completed basic work, it is time to start to think about working for others and undertaking more advanced work. At a certain stage, you should feel intuitively that the focus of your work should be directed outward and not inward. This is a natural step for anyone on a spiritual path. In the classic hero's journey, the hero returns with gifts or wisdom for the benefit of all. In this section we start to prepare you to work with others.

Working with Others

Here is a general structure that can be used for healing sessions with other people:

1. **Permission.** Obtain permission from the person to heal them (if it cannot be assumed).

2. **Discussion.** Ask what they want. Let them talk, which is part of the healing process.

3. **Diagnosis.** Perform divination to get a diagnosis and advice on which modality to use.

4. **Explanation.** Provide a basic explanation of the healing and what to expect.

5. **Participation.** Explain they are an active participant and to be open to receive healing.

6. **Physical contact.** Explain any contact required and confirm the person does not object.

7. **Q&A.** Let the person ask questions before, during, and at the end of a session.

8. **Tools.** Use a drum or rattle to journey or enter trance, not a recording.

9. **Duration.** A normal session will usually be an hour but may take longer.

10. **Follow-up work.** After a session advise the person how to integrate healing, if follow-up work is needed, and the timing for this. Let a person contact you if they need help.

Healing Guidelines

There are some key ethical considerations and other guidelines relevant for shamanic healing:

1. **Referral to medical professionals.** Medical problems should be referred to a medical doctor, psychiatrist, or psychologist. Some diseases must be officially notified.

2. **Licenses.** For some work licenses are required at local or state level.

3. **Permission.** You need permission to perform healing. If a person is in a coma, journey to their soul for guidance. For a child, you need to get permission from both parents.

4. **Approach.** Act professionally and responsibly, treating others with care, patience, tolerance, kindness and compassion, and giving comfort and support. Be open-minded, non-judgemental, and learn to be a good listener. Treat information in confidence. Do not take advantage of others and avoid inappropriate personal relationships. Do not let your ego get in the way. Only give healing when you are fit to do so.

5. **Attachment to outcome.** Do not be attached to outcome, which may interfere with healing. An outcome may be what is needed, not necessarily what you or others want.

Code of Conduct

A Code of Conduct should be used by a practitioner: either one published by a relevant body or an individual one. Example codes that can be used as a basis for your own include:

- https://www.shamanism.org/resources/ethics-legal.html
- https://shamanicpractice.org/code-of-ethics/
- http://www.councilforhealing.org/About.html

A Code of Conduct may cover guidelines, qualifications, advertising, behavior, interaction with clients, working with other professionals, and working at a hospital or hospice.

Pro Tips

The following tips are provided:

1. **Legality of actions.** Healers must comply with criminal and civil law as it relates to healing, including making prescriptions or advertising claims for some conditions. You are advised to research and understand the legal framework in your location.

2. **Law affecting alternative medicine.** Practices considered "alternative medicine" may or may not be regulated by law. Even where forms of alternative medicine are not regulated by legislation, some laws may have an indirect effect on these practices.

3. **Actions to avoid.** Healers should not prescribe or sell remedies, herbs, supplements, oils, or other products unless they have received training and/or qualifications that allow them to do so. There are different rules depending on whether products are classed as medicines, cosmetics, or foodstuffs.

4. **Insurance.** There may or may not be a compulsory requirement for alternative medicine practitioners to take out malpractice or other forms of insurance.

5. **Data privacy.** In most jurisdictions there are data privacy and protection regulations. These relate to any data from which a person's identify may be identified and apply to any person that collects, holds,

processes or uses such data. If data is held about a person, they usually have a right to obtain a copy of data and make corrections to it. If you operate a website you should usually have some form of data privacy statement in it confirming your compliance with legislation and explaining what data you collect, how you use it, in what circumstances it may be disclosed, how long it is retained, and how people can request access to their data.

LONG-DISTANCE HEALING

Healing may be performed via long-distance healing for a person by an individual or by a group. A person does not need to be in the physical presence of a practitioner for healing to be effective. Long-distance healing is done in the spiritual reality aspect of the middle world, which allows for healing to be done remotely. Group work can be done in person, or by members of an email group who receive healing requests and do the work individually.

What Can be Healed Remotely

Most healing modalities can be used remotely. Those that require use of physical objects or materials cannot be done in the usual manner, but you can still do work in spiritual reality using different methods or the spirit of the objects or materials normally used.

When Long-distance Healing is Relevant

The use of long-distance healing is particularly useful in the following situations:

1. **Convenience.** Where a person cannot easily visit a practitioner, perhaps due to living in a remote location, or travel easily (perhaps if they are handicapped) or where there is not a practitioner in their local area.

2. **Preference.** Where a person would prefer to have the work done remotely for some other reason, for instance if they do not feel comfortable meeting practitioners in person, if they cannot be in proximity to others due to having an illness of some kind, or if they want to receive healing from a particular practitioner.

3. **Timing.** The work can be scheduled when convenient for an individual healer or a group of people, who can work at different times for a client.

4. **Power.** Where the combined power of a group needs to be used. This is especially relevant where a serious illness is being addressed and/or a miraculous cure is sought.

5. **Animals.** Long-distance healing can also be used on animals, where it may be even more difficult for such healing to be done in person, especially if the animal is in a zoo or is a wild animal in nature.

Long-distance Healing Process

Long-distance healing is done in two ways: where a person requests healing directly from a practitioner, or where a person requests healing from a group that offers remote healing.

In the first case, a person can discuss long-distance healing with a practitioner to understand what work can be done and how it will be performed. They can ask questions about the work and receive answers from the practitioner. The practitioner journeys in the middle world to the person's location and performs healing in the same way they would if the person were present, with any needed modifications. The practitioner can ask their helping spirits or power animals to assist in healing. They then report the results of the healing work, any other recommendations or advice, and the results of any divination requested to the person who has received the healing.

Alternatively, healing may be performed, and the results relayed to the person receiving healing via video or voice conferencing technology. The person receiving the healing may then also ask questions about the healing or follow-up work that they need to do.

In the second case, a person provides basic details to a person who will forward them to a healing group or may submit them directly to the group. Usually the person's name, location, and details of what healing they would like are asked for. The group then performs the healing, together or individually. Again, the results of healing or other information may be shared with the person who requested the healing. This may be provided by the individual healers directly to the person concerned or may be collated by the person who was contacted about the healing. The latter may be appropriate if group members wish to remain anonymous.

If a person does not know what needs to be done, or does not want to discuss this, they can request that the practitioner or group do the work by performing a divination to find out what healing is needed, and then performing healing appropriate for the person.

Key Ritual: Journey to Perform Long-distance Healing Requested for a Person

The intention is to journey to perform long-distance for somebody that has requested healing. What they have asked for is described to the healing participants.

Mark

> I receive an email requesting help, stop what I am doing, close my eyes, and journey to the middle world. I call my power animals to join me and we all fly together across the Pacific Ocean to California. We descend into the room where the person who will receive healing is lying. I am aware of other spirits in the room who make room for us to approach the person who is to be healed.
>
> The power animals position themselves around her, hold space and perform their own healing. I extend my arms with the hands palm down toward her, pull spirit power down and extend white light rays from my hands that enter the center of her body and join. An intense white energy ball is created that spreads out to fill her body, healing and empowering her. I note a message received from spirit that I will later communicate to the person using the personal email address that was provided.

How to Do the Key Ritual

This information, and permission to do the work, is typically obtained beforehand (often in an email sent to a healing group). People then journey to do the healing required themselves as guided or with a helping spirit (or sometimes the spirit does the healing). Where a group is working together physically one person will drum or rattle.

A person provides a practitioner with their name, location, permission for long-distance healing to occur, what they seek healing for, and whether they are open to receiving divination or other messages that practitioners receive. If an individual is performing the healing, they journey to the person's location in the spiritual reality aspect of the middle world and perform healing as they normally would but without physical reality interaction. Their spirits may help.

If a group of healers is involved, the practitioner communicates details of the healing request to the practitioners concerned. Often this is a closed email group of people who know each other well and who will keep client details and the results of healing work confidential. The group members perform the work when convenient for them, usually alone. They may involve a local group of fellow practitioners in work if relevant and the group agrees to this.

If it has been requested, any divination or other messages are communicated back to the practitioner who raised the long-distance healing request, or to the client directly.

Other Rituals

Other rituals that you can perform include: journey to find a person who needs long-distance healing, journey to diagnose and heal illness in a person's body, and remote healing with a crystal.

Journey to Find a Person Who Needs Long-distance Healing

The intention is to journey to a hospice, hospital ICU or other location to find a person who wants healing, and to deliver healing. How do we get permission for this work? There might be a spirit taking care of the person and we can ask this spirit (as long as we are sure this is an authentic message). We can also journey to the person's spirit and ask them if they want healing done and what they would like.

> #### *Jean*
> There is someone in bed and a spirit standing next to them. They have already died. I asked for permission to do healing and he was desperate because he wanted to live again.

I asked what happened and it turned out there was a family argument, and he had a heart attack. My teacher told me to send him a symbol, so I sent a healing symbol to him. The other part of the healing was for him to realize he had died, and this is a natural process. I saw him going into a tunnel filled with light and disappear.

Journey to Diagnose and Heal Illness in a Person's Body

The intention is to journey through another person's crown chakra into their body, search out any illness, and then perform healing as you are guided. When you have finished, exit the person's body through the crown chakra again.

Maya

It was so crazy; I was laughing. I went into your head. I was a little person, and my horse was with me. This was just fun. Your eyes were tired, they were strained. So, we healed both of them, and then we kept going. Mostly everything was good. There was a little bit of carpal tunnel stuff, is that a nerve? On each side it was a little sore, like inflamed, so we healed the sides of whatever it is.

Lungs were fine, heart was fine, the guts had a little something, it was a little spot. I don't like random white spots. It didn't have a nice feeling, so we healed it. Then the Horse and I expanded until we filled you and we were just like glowing inside of you so your whole body was glowing. Like one big star full of brightness. The cells were all invited to be at a very healthy level and then we left.

Remote Healing with a Crystal

The intention is to use a crystal to perform long-distance healing on a person. There are several ways in which crystals can be used in remote healing. In one method the image of a person who is to be healed is placed in the crystal and a healing ceremony performed focusing on that image with the intention that the person is healed remotely.

In another the crystal is asked to retrieve the image of a person who is to be healed (we can infer that the crystal spirit journeys to the person to do this) and the crystal is asked to heal the image of the person. A variation of this would be to send the crystal to the remote person and ask its spirit to heal them.

In the example below the practitioner merges with the crystal and travels in the middle world to a person that is to receive healing. Then the healing is performed as guided. Let the crystal inform you how the healing will be done. You can do this ritual with or without journeying; here it is done without. You can touch or hold the crystal if this helps you to focus.

Maya

I felt myself go into the crystal and we were one. Then we went to the part of the person that has the bad cells, and at first the crystal would kind of shine and kind of made all the cells happy, I don't know how else to describe it, bringing happiness. Then we brought the cells out that were not as happy with us to the brothers and sisters of this crystal and they kind of like sort of sang and changed the cells. Then we went back with the cells, put them back in the body and then that was it and we came back.

My intention was to heal the cells. What I think happened is it allows the cells to see that they can go back to normal, they can be normal again, if they want to. It doesn't necessarily mean they changed, but it just means that maybe it is kind of like a little "Hey, this is how you are functioning, and this is how you could function, so you are invited to function this way again."

Pro Tips

The following tips are provided:

1. **Personal information.** Make sure personal data remains confidential. A person's address or other details can be provided to a closed email group whose members will perform healing, but not to a public email group or to a social media forum.

2. **Intention.** The intention must be clearly stated for practitioners who do the healing.

3. **Time.** In spiritual reality time in non-linear. This makes it possible to deliver healing in the past or future as well as the present, or for a

group to work at different times and have an effect at a specific point in time, for instance just before a medical procedure.

4. **Experience.** The person receiving the healing may or may not have sensations during the healing, which may of course not be at a set time (especially if many healers are doing healing at different times).

5. **Death is healing.** Sometimes the appropriate healing is for a person to die and a practitioner helps to ease this process in any way that is relevant.

EARTH HEALING

Earth healing restores harmony and balance to the earth by healing its energetic structures and alleviating problems caused by geopathic stress and human activities. This involves working with different types of spirits and rituals using modified versions of healing modalities used for human healing, together with additional modalities specific to earth healing. Earth healing typically involves working in the middle world in both physical and spiritual reality.

Geomancy involves rituals for auspicious site or building design, restoring vitality to the earth, and divination using markings on the ground or patterns in soil, sand, or rock. Geomancers work with directions and physical or non-physical landscape aspects, including working with nature spirits. Similar techniques are thus used in geomancy and shamanism.

The Earth's Energetic Structure

The earth's energetic structure is complex and comprises lines within which energy moves, and locations where lines cross or power is concentrated. These affect living beings positively or negatively and can also be affected by human activities. Intersections can cause illness. Key components of the earth's energetic structure include geomagnetic grids, fault lines, underground water streams, power places, ley lines, and artificial electromagnetic grids.

Two geomagnetic grids are produced by the earth's geomagnetic field, aligned to cardinal and cross-quarter directions. These produce electromagnetic waves that oscillate between the earth and atmosphere regulating sleep, hormones, and the menstrual cycle. Geological fault lines and weather phenomena can affect this process. Underground water streams may cross and amplify grids. Black streams carry unhealthy energy and white streams healthy energy.

Power places are where power is concentrated and may be sacred sites. Ley lines are energy meridians (neutral, positive, or negative) aligned to underground streams, power places, or sacred sites. Stones can be used to create lines and connect to power and metal stakes can be used to divert or stop lines. At vortexes energy radiates from the earth or lines converge creating a whirlpool that is negative (grounding), positive (power source), or neutral (calming).

Artificial electromagnetic grids can affect your health if you are exposed to strong fields. Electrical and electromagnetic pollution can move in underground streams. Human activities can also cause energetic imprints, which can be positive or negative.

Geopathic Stress

Geopathic stress caused by negative energy results in physical, emotional, or mental issues, including illness or fertility and sleep problems. It may be the result of disturbed energy in the environment or the presence of artificial structures. Geopathic stress is dealt with by avoiding it by relocating buildings or sleep areas, diverting it using techniques like earth acupuncture, neutralizing it with stones or protective objects like amulets, relocating negative flows to a safe location like a water body with no human activity, or healing it.

Geopathic Stress Indicators

The presence of geopathic stress can be inferred from indicators, or via journeys or divination. Indicators include increases in crime or accident rates or avoiding stress in sleep positions. Animal behavior can also indicate stress. Some animals thrive on stress (cats, owls, crows, snakes, slugs, snails, ants, termites, wasps, and bees), but it makes others sick or injury prone (horses and cows). Some trees thrive on it (oak, ash, and elder) while it may cause dead spots in hedges, trees, or grass, or a drop in crop production. Geopathic stress also causes damage or electrical problems in buildings where it is carried by steel frames, wiring, and pipes. It can cause increased paranormal activity and disturb spirits.

Earth Healing Process

Land can heal itself over time, but healing rituals you perform can accelerate this. If the land has been damaged for some time, the spirits of the land may have left. You can heal the earth, spirits of place, land, or buildings by balancing, removing, retrieving, and inserting energy.

Techniques used are based on the healing modalities described previously, such as releasing energy created by violence or trauma (extraction), conducting negative energy into the earth to be neutralized (terrapomp), soul retrieval for the earth if spirits of place to restore vitality to a location, and psychopomp of ghosts to stop energetic patterns affecting living beings. In addition, advanced techniques such as removing curses from land can be used.

You can also work with energetic imprints (removing or inserting them); transmute toxins; correct or restore energy in ley lines, vortexes, or power places; balance elemental energy at a location; work with land spirits to restore or insert vitality to a location; remove invasive species; perform earth acupuncture (needles may be left in position as temples, sculptures, standing stones, or trees); use bonfires to perform moxibustion healing; or use ceremonies and rituals to obtain permission for construction from land spirits, prepare a site, and mark activities such as ground-breaking, topping out, or opening.

Other things we can do include:

- Physical and/or energetic regeneration of the land.

- Acknowledging past mistakes by humans and apologizing for this, but it may take time before spirits are willing to let you help.

- Holding solar festivals on land and including relevant earth healing rituals.

- Infusion the land with light from the sun (or moon) to clear and empower it.

- Healing spirits of the land, or spirits of animals and plants that live there.

- Re-establishing eldership or guardianship.

- Scattering seeds, or tending the wild, and doing this intentionally as a land healer.

Key Ritual: Journey to Work with Power Centers

The intention is to journey to a power center to find out about it and how to work with it.

James

I went to a lake in Hokkaido near a dormant volcano. There is a vortex in the lake. There are plans to build there and spirits had left because of lack of acknowledgement of the Ainu people and bear spirits. They work with the vortex and if it is not restored the positive potential of the area to be a healing area will not be realized. They said I can make a simple shrine with rock and twig and invite spirits back.

Before the Ainu people helped the flow of energy, and they were happy that I came to work on that. I gathered energy into a bag, we sat around a fire and they said I had to put it in the fire. It will become ash and we can put that on the earth. I saw a bear shaman and we started communicating. I saw the energy of the place having more life. The bear shaman slashed me across the face with a claw, so it was bleeding and pulled me toward him and put our cheeks together, so we are connected, blood brothers.

There was imagery that nature would come back in that area. A female spirit came. The four of us did a fire ritual. I was aware there was another shrine halfway up the mountain that was disturbed and I did work with that. It seems once you start to do work with one there is a domino effect with interconnected shrines. I got a sense that a downpour of spirits like a river would start. This process was quite powerful.

How to Do the Key Ritual

Journey with the intention of going to a power center or ask a helping spirit to take you to one. You should qualify this to go to a positive power center. You will often fly to such a place and view it from above, where you see an energy vortex emerging from the earth, looking like a whirlpool. Ask one of your helping spirits or a spirit at the power center to tell you about it and how you might work with it. It may be possible to step into the power center and receive a healing or empowerment.

Other Rituals

Other rituals that you can perform include: journey to understand the earth's energetic structure, journey to perform extraction healing on the earth, journey to perform terrapomp healing, journey to perform soul retrieval for the earth, journey to work with energetic imprints in the earth, and journey to transform toxins in the earth.

Other modalities that are described above can be explored with helping spirits. You can also perform healing for other planets, for the moon, sun, or stars using similar techniques. You can also perform rituals to work with underground water streams, balance energy fields, or restore a spirit to a location.

Journey to Understand the Earth's Energetic Structure

The intention is to journey to find out about the earth's energetic structure and how you can work with it. As well as geomagnetic grids, you may learn about earth meridians or chakras.

> #### Lilian
>
> I saw meridians like a web around the earth. Where the crust is thin you feel energy more. There are more white lines than black. Earth meridians are affected by thoughts. It is alive. The earth has inter-dimensional chakras, some fading out into space. The one I need to know about is at the center and is the earth's heart chakra. We can connect to it through our heart chakra. I asked about healing and it said for meridian lines I can use sound and do a layout of bowls on a line and play sound into the ground.

Journey to Perform Extraction Healing on the Earth

The intention is to journey is to learn how to perform extraction healing on the earth to remove negative energetic imprints and other energies, in spiritual or physical reality.

Ann

> Two power animals and I went to a desert. A spirit cut the
> earth energetically with her hands, the earth lifted up and
> out rushed this red and brown stuff and went up. That
> went on for a long time. When that had all gone, she told
> us to put our hands up and did the same and white light
> came down like a vortex, a healing energy. They the earth
> came together and meshed, and she told us to get down
> and smooth and seal it.

Journey to Perform Terrapomp Healing

The intention is to journey to find an energetic pattern like a negative
thought form that is causing negative effects to living beings and conduct
this into the earth to be transformed. You can use relevant symbols associated with transformation like wells and cauldrons.

Ann

> I was taken out into a large wilderness area. Two panthers
> appeared and merged, and I got on their back. We traveled
> a long time and then stopped. They used their claws to
> scratch at the earth and I got down and joined them. We
> scratched and they asked me to scoop it. I scooped it all up
> and there was like an earthenware bucket that I put it in.
>
> I got back onto the back of the animal and we went to an
> empty volcano and were really deep inside it. When we got
> down to the bottom I got off and there was like water that
> was fire, a small lake of fire. I was told to put the energy in
> there and I did that. Then I came back to the wilderness
> and was told the job was done.

Journey to Perform Soul Retrieval for the Earth

The intention is to perform soul retrieval for the earth. Part(s) could have
been lost due to events like meteor impacts and could be anywhere in physical or spiritual reality. Parts need to be persuaded to come back and then
brought back and inserted into Mother Earth. Parts will be quite powerful
and need to be convinced you are powerful enough to work with them.

Ryan

She gave me a sliver of energy which was a white crystal
wand with a gilded handle. She said we would be connected by the light of it, "shine it toward me and all with
return." I held up the wand then twiddled it and struck
up a song asking parts to come back from where they are
hiding and return to Gaia. Light like stars was shooting
into the wand and it was getting heavy. I aimed it back
to Gaia and the energy shot back together with the wand
itself. I returned and she expressed gratitude.

Journey to Work with Energetic Imprints in the Earth

The intention is to extract a negative energetic imprint from a location and
insert a positive energetic imprint to replace it. We need to decide where we
are going to go or ask to be guided, how we are going to do the extraction,
how this energy is to be transmuted, how the insertion will be done, and
also who we need to obtain permission from for such work.

The extraction is done as we are guided. To transmute energy, we can
send it to Mother Earth herself or to an alternate like the sun. It is appropriate to send energy to the earth as we are removing negative energy from a
particular location which she can re-use.

For the positive imprint we have to think about its nature and how it is
constructed. This imprint is a pattern which will enable energy in the location where it is used to come into harmony and balance. The energy may
have an inherent pattern, or we may construct the pattern with a specific
intention. We can ask how the imprint should be made and inserted.

Maya

I flew to Florida and saw a man hanging from a tree. He
was the victim of a lynching. I realized he was still there
so my vulture and I psychopomped him. At first, he didn't
want to go. He was angry and there was lots of darkness,
which I could understand. So, I talked to him a little bit
and said, "Let's go look and then you can decide." I knew
he was going to go. He agreed and we flew together. He
went inside the lower world.

This was where a lot of people were lynched. It was just anger living there. The energy of anger had impacted the animals and everything. We went back to the spot and it still had negative energy. I was directed by my horse spirit to just lift it up. I asked if Gaia would take it back. She opened and I just pushed it down into the earth and then closed it up. I asked if the area needed to be clean, but it is fine. The space was happy, normal, vibrant nature space.

Journey to Transform Toxins in the Earth

The intention is to journey to a spirit to learn how to effect change in the environment by transmuting toxic substances into neutral ones. This can be via direct transformation of a substance or alchemical inner transformation of us which is then reflected in the outer world by us seeding the outer environment from the transmuted essence within us.

Permission is trickier as the effects of the work we will do are potentially more widespread and will therefore affect a larger number of beings. We also need to be guided as to what sort of toxin we will work with. Potentials include pollution, noise, environmental toxins, social media, etc.

If somebody has created something that has negative effects, do we need permission to change that to make it better? Of course, our idea of change may not be what others agree with. In each situation we have to decide if we want to intentionally perform work. Ask if it feels right, try to qualify your intention to encourage a positive outcome, and confirm a course of action with spirit.

Maya

I went in and I was like social media stuff and it was really interesting because it was sludge all over the US, just nasty, gray-black sludge. A box appeared. Some of my power animals were there. I had to scoop up the sludge without touching it.

It was cool because the hands became sort of like glowy things of protection, and I scooped it up and put it in the earth. They said, "Burn it." So, I said okay and created a fire and it burned. Then we opened it and smoke came out.

I said the smoke has to go somewhere, where is it going. It went to the universe to help create something new. It is going to be disseminated to create something else.

In the vacuum that was left behind from all that going I took starlight and put it there. I am like, why am I taking starlight and why is it healing. They said it was re-using their vibrations, the intention of the starlight was to raise up only those for whom it would work in their greatest good, and those who can't handle whatever it is would be as they are and that's it.

They said, "That box is yours now, you know what to do with it, put it in your chest and keep it for next time."

Pro Tips

The following tips are provided:

1. **Confirmation.** Confirm with spirits of place or your helping spirits that healing is required. Make sure issues are not natural processes that do not need healing.

2. **Permission.** You get permission from owners, residents, and spirit(s) of place.

3. **Context.** Look at a place's history and current problems. Ask how people, animals and plants are affected and if issues are seen in one place or at set times. Identify patterns and the origin of issues. Try to remove clear energetic patterns so issues do not recur.

4. **Timing.** Rituals may be aligned to sun and moon cycles, seasons or celestial events. Determine the best time for work using published information or by asking spirit.

5. **Participation.** Hold a ceremony and perform healing. Include owners, residents, or workers in such ceremony if possible as this helps with healing integration. Explain relevant aspects of the work to them and look for opportunities to involve them.

DREAMS

We often do not understand dreams and only remember nightmares. Dream interpretation is usually by interpreting symbols from a dream dictionary, which may not be relevant to your personal symbology. The same symbols are seen in journeys and dreams, and dreamwork is another tool for shamanic work. Shamanic cultures see dreams as a separate reality and work actively with their dreams, from which they obtain power, knowledge, and healing.

You spend a third of your life asleep; some part of which you can work consciously with dreams. You dream during the stage of sleep called REM (Rapid Eye Movement), which occurs mainly during the final two hours of sleep. This means that, if you live to be seventy, you will spend some six years of your life in REM sleep, which could be used for dreamwork.

There are several types of dream:

- **Ordinary dreams.** Where you are an observer of events with little control.

- **Vivid dreams.** Powerful dreams that contain key information and are remembered.

- **Nightmares.** Frightening dreams which may recur.

- **Lucid dreams.** Where you "wake up" in the dream and can take control of events.

- **Waking dreams.** A dream while awake, such as a daydream.

- **Visions.** A vivid waking dream that may include empowerment by spirit.

- **Group dreams.** Where more than one person works collectively in dreams.

- **Universal dreams.** Dreams shared by all members of a culture or by all humanity.

Shamanic Dreaming

There are different theories on the nature dreams and the dream world. These usually have a psychological basis, where dreams are associated with our subconscious or with a collective unconscious. A shamanic view of dreams has some different views:

1. The dream world and dreams are real. The dream world is part of spiritual reality.

2. Physical reality is a manifestation of dreams by humans, spirits, and nature.

3. In dreams you can receive teaching, divination, and healing for yourself or others.

4. You can work with spirit helpers and specialist dream spirits, who may give you dreams.

5. Dream symbols can be used to interpret or trigger dreams.

6. Journeying is intentional dreaming.

Dreams are created or influenced by personal helping spirits or suffering spirits. The latter can produce nightmares, which are indicative of a spirit that you can help heal. Interaction with spirits can be direct, where they enter the dream to provide teaching, healing, or initiation, or indirect, where they influence dream content. Shamans respect dreams as they contain messages from spirit. In traditional societies shamans work with their own or other's dreams.

Shamanic dreaming involves interaction with spirits while you are dreaming and includes collective dream practices. This can involve rituals such as meeting others while dreaming to share a dream. It also includes larger dreams that guide our collective destiny. Such dreams can be tended by individuals who protect and serve the dream. Shamans also dream the future, which is one way of co-creating physical reality with spirit.

Exploring the Dream World

If you can achieve a lucid dream state you can interact with the dream and explore the dream world, moving around, working with others, and making changes to a dream. In dreams we are not restricted by physical laws and, as in a journey, can fly, shape-shift, and time travel.

You can create objects, people, places, or events in a dream, or use portals to locations where people or things exist. Dream objects like doors or mirrors can be used as portals by intending to go somewhere and stepping into the object. You can also teleport by closing your eyes, intending that you are somewhere else, and opening your eyes to manifest that location.

Dream characters may be mental creations, other people, or spirits. Everything is sentient, although may have varying awareness levels. Those you meet in a dream may not understand they are in a dream or be able to communicate. You should try to ascertain who dream people are, why they are there, and if they can help you and/or you can help them.

Dream Healing

You can give or receive healing in a dream, which can manifest in healing in physical reality. This is similar to long-distance healing, with dreaming and journeying being similar activities, both of which occur in spiritual reality. If you are lucid in a dream, you can give healing using normal healing modalities. Shadow or soul parts may appear in your dreams.

Other healing approaches can also be used in dreams. You can create or visit a dream clinic or healing temple or use a healing agent or device such as healing light or some sort of healing tool. You can also ask a dream or a spirit to send a healer to you. As you visit and use healing locations in dreams, they get stronger. Before sleeping you can visualize a healing you want to receive, or a person that you want to heal.

Working with Dreams

Shamanic dreamwork aims to explore and use dreams, understand the spirits and energy in dreams, interpret dream contents, and facilitate integration, resolution, or some other benefit for the dreamer or the community.

Things beneficial to dreaming include spending a relevant number of hours sleeping, not consuming alcohol before sleeping (which reduces the time you spend in REM sleep), and using positive affirmations before you go to sleep, such as "I remember my dreams."

Remembering, recording, and interpreting dreams encourages them, and the more attention we give dreams the more spirit uses them to communicate with us. You can work with dreams via keeping a dream journal, dream recall, dream incubation, dream interpretation, working with nightmares, dream re-entry, dream creativity, dream tools, and lucid dreaming. You can also make changes in a dream with an intention; this causes related changes in physical reality.

Keeping a dream journal helps you to discover what goes on in your dreams, improves your dream recall, and lets you look for patterns and trends in dreams. A good practice is to note keywords that describe the dream experience and use these as prompts to recall details. You can also draw a dream. Note key symbols, objects, places, people, and events in a dream.

Dream incubation is done by deciding a dream intention before going to sleep. This can refer to a spirit you want to meet, who you can ask for information or healing. You can also intend that you have a lucid dream. In an incubated dream you may recall your intention, which may itself trigger lucidity. Write a dream intention and the dream results in your dream journal.

Dream interpretation uses the same techniques as journey interpretation. Symbols appear in dreams, often placed there by spirits to aid communication, and have the same meaning in dreams and journeys. You can interpret scenes and combine these into an overall meaning, or journey to a spirit or work with a dream practitioner to help interpret a dream. Identifying symbols helps you see them the next time they appear in a dream, which may trigger lucidity.

Nightmares may relate to stress, illness, shadow parts or things you are avoiding. They can contain guidance and allow you to face your fears. If you acknowledge a nightmare and face it, you remove its power over you; if you avoid and repress it, it will recur. Ask a nightmare what it is trying to teach you and focus on changing yourself not the dream. Nightmares may be helped by smudging a sleep area or calling a spirit to protect and help you in dreams. Dream eaters are supernatural animals a dreamer asks to protect them or to eat nightmares.

Dream re-entry is done by setting an intention to do so before sleeping or by entering a dream via a journey. It allows us to get clarity on dream meaning, to ask a dream character or spirit to explain something, or to continue a dream from the point you woke up to get other insights.

Dream creativity can be done by making artwork, working on projects in a dream or using a dream to prototype work. When making artwork you can use tools like brushes and paint or intend to manifest works directly.

You can place yourself in an artwork or story to experience it, have a singer or band perform a composition, or use a similar mechanism for other types of creativity. You can also create a dream studio or dream library.

Dream tools can be created in a dream, such as a dream wand or an entrance for spirit helpers. You can also work with the spirit of physical reality tools in dream. Dream makers are tools that promote dreams. Dream catchers are tools that filter out bad dreams, with good dreams passing to the dreamer. Dream catchers are often placed above a bed or crib.

Lucid dreams can happen spontaneously or be induced. You may be aware you are dreaming but not able to influence or have full control over a dream. Most people can dream lucidly with some training. In a lucid dream you can face your fears, phobias, anxieties or nightmares. You can also heal past trauma or experience things without being controlled by your ego. Lucid dreams are a source of power, and lucid dreamers often have mystical experiences. Mastering lucid dreaming is an essential step to shamanic dreaming.

A number of things can help encourage lucid dreaming, including keeping a dream journal, practising dream recall, clearing stress and quietening your mind prior to sleeping, having a strong intention to be lucid in a dream (such as "I will be lucid in my dreams tonight"), and waking up six hours into the sleep cycle and going back to sleep during a REM sleep period. The most useful techniques are performing reality checks and using objects to trigger lucidity.

A reality check is based on identifying one or more symbols you have seen in dreams and that you can also experience while awake. When you see the symbol in physical reality you as the question "Am I dreaming?" You will know that you are not. This encourages you to ask the same question if you see the symbol when you are dreaming, which may trigger lucidity. Spirit may put the symbol in your dreams to help. Symbols could include seeing a specific animal, hearing someone call your name, opening a door, and seeing the moon. The more often you do a reality check while awake, the more likely it is you will do it in a dream.

Using objects to trigger lucidity involves selecting a stone such as a crystal that you can hold in your hand and having the intentions of being lucid in your dream and for the stone to accompany you into the dream. Hold the stone as you fall asleep. With practice the stone should begin to appear in your dreams, at which point seeing it should trigger the lucid state.

You can confirm that you are dreaming by taking an action such as seeing if you can pass your hand through a solid object, checking your reflection or looking at your hands or feet to see if they are normal, or trying to fly.

It is difficult at first to maintain a lucid state, and if distracted you can easily fall back into a non-lucid state. If you become lucid, try to maintain the lucid state by interacting with the dream, reminding yourself you are in a dream, and enabling multiple senses to help focus.

Through lucid dreaming, practitioners can meet while dreaming at a specific place in physical or spiritual reality to perform group rituals.

Key Ritual: Journey to Understand Dreams

The intention is to journey to a power animal, teaching spirit or specialist dream spirit and obtain information about what dreams are and how to work with them.

Sam

I went to the underworld and was flying with my animals in a dark forest. We flew up a hill, there is a castle at the top. I know it is the castle of the witch, but I do not need to meet her this time. In the hallway is a very beautiful lady in a white dress.

She said she is the pet bird of the witch; she is a bird in the daytime and becomes a lady at night. She said, just like my dreams, when she is a bird, she can't remember the nighttime, but when she is a lady, she can remember the bird. When dreaming the bird is free and it is itself.

She said it is better not to try to control things because many people control with fear. If you want to control, control with love. She said, to work with dreams I should set a clear intention when going to sleep. I should write down the dream, get the message inside, and say goodbye to it.

How to Do the Key Ritual

Here you can journey to a helping spirit, a specialist teaching spirit, an archetypal dream spirit, or another spirit that you encounter in such a dream. They may give you advice and/or you may need to interpret the events in the journey.

Other Rituals

Other rituals that you can perform include: journey to the Dream Matrix, journey to the Dream Weaver, journey to learn how to have lucid dreams, and journey to clear the dreams of the dead from the dream world.

You can also journey to learn how to dream lucidly, to re-enter a dream, to interpret a dream, to face and understand a nightmare, to ask for a vision, to understand a universal dream, to create spirit dream guardians for others, and to learn how to heal in a dream, or from the dream to heal someone in physical reality.

Journey to the Dream Matrix

The intention is to journey to base energy from which the dream world and dreams are made, to understand the nature of this energy, and perhaps how you might use it yourself.

> *Sue*
>
> There was so much going on all the time. I started off and there were wild spirit horses running past me; I was walking through the middle of them to get down into the matrix. That was pretty powerful.
>
> Then I saw so many different visions, structured and unstructured, swimming, floating, visions of sky, some-times lots of people involved, sometimes people behind doors having dreams or conversations, sometimes groups of people doing stuff, sometimes completely silent, some-times going down tunnels. It was really amazing.
>
> I was trying to find out more about what it was and how you could use it. To me, it is accessible wherever and whenever you need it. Things I was experiencing there I experience daily, and it is a place to process emotions and

conversations in a faster way to make decisions. It is also a place to create things, to mould things as you wanted if you took a conscious part in the process.

Journey to the Dream Weaver

The intention is to journey to the Dream Weaver, an archetypal spirit responsible for dreams from who we can find out about the dream world and dreams, and how to work with them.

Lilian

I really liked the space of the Dream Weaver. It seemed very familiar. It was like a Tim Burton movie. I was going down a silvery-black track with the full moon and very whimsical trees. The Dream Weaver first appeared as a sound all around telling me things. It said this is a world of magic, but also a real world.

You can plot intentions in this world and have the intentions become real. You can also bring problems to the dream world, look at them from another angle, and solve them. I wanted to see the Dream Weaver and saw a frog with a crown on it like in the fairy tale. They said, "Go ahead and give the frog a kiss."

I said, "I would rather not," but I might have.

Journey to Learn How to Have Lucid Dreams

The intention is to journey to a helping or teaching spirit to ask for advice about things we can do so that we will be able to have lucid dreams.

Jean

I asked, "How I can have lucid dreams?" My spirit teacher gave me a word, *brave*, and I asked, "What do you mean by this?"

She explained, "If there is no fear inside you there is no blockage, all of your energies can flow so that you can control what you want to happen."

I always dream about entities attacking me, so I asked about them. She said, "Those dreams of being attacked are usually self-reflections. You may have some energy in your body which you have to release."

Journey to Clear the Dreams of the Dead from the Dream World

The intention is to clear dream memories of the dead from the collective dream space, so they do not interfere with the dreams of the living. This can release and transmute dream energy. It can also release spirits that were stuck in the dream. This may include the spirits of the dead who were having the dream, who can then be helped by psychopomp healing.

Lilian

It was like being in the clouds in a plane. We came to a place that looked like a sheet of ice. Underneath it was bubbles that had frozen and collected and couldn't escape. These were the dreams of the dead that were stuck. I had to bring them to the surface and crack it open. There was a huge rushing of the bubbles to the surface, they rose up and broke and people fell down from them.

There were crowds of them. They were desperately clawing as they thought they were going to die, but then they realized they are no longer alive when they reached the ground. They were stunned. I asked Archangel Michael to help me and we set up the light and with the top of his sword he created a huge portal which the people went through. They started out as old and incapacitated but, as they entered the light, they became whole.

Pro Tips

The following tips are provided:

1. **Serious intent.** Dream work should be for serious intentions, not frivolous pursuits.

2. **Other people.** People we meet in dreams may be spirits or living people and we should treat them with respect. Real people we meet in a dream may not be lucid.

3. **Closure.** Meeting and communicating with people in a dream, who may be dead or alive, can result in profound healing and closure in relationship issues.

4. **Energy indicators.** Things stuck in a dream may indicate where you are stuck in your life. Where energy is moving it may refer to something that is coming into your life.

5. **Dreaming and dying.** Lucid dreaming can teach us techniques which will be useful when we die and can be used to facilitate our crossing to where we should go.

CREATIVITY

Everyone is naturally creative; you do not need to be artistic or have special skills to be creative. To shamans, creativity is a fundamental aspect of reality. Given your source connection to spirit, your creative potential is unlimited. Creativity lets you make tangible things such as artwork and intangible things such as theories. Journeys and dreams can connect you to creative sources and provide inspiration in their content. The act of journeying or dreaming also helps to make you more creative. Creations can also be healing.

You create by removing creative blocks, being in a state of *flow*, and accessing sources of inspiration. Creative blocks can be imposed by you or others and may arise from past lives or ancestral influences. You may worry what others will think, fear making a mistake, or feel you are not able to create. Flow is a state of connection of body, mind, and spirit achieved by entering a trance state and being open to receive inspiration. From creative sources you can access mythical knowledge, archetypes, symbols, wisdom, and inspiration.

Shamanic Creativity

Journeying lets you develop your creative potential, get ideas and inspiration, create things in spiritual reality and obtain teachings. You can work with teachers such as:

- Helping and teaching spirits.
- Spirit muses.

- The spirits of creators, like a dead author, artist or musician.

- Other specialist teaching spirits such as a spirit librarian or editor.

- The spirits of creations (which may or may not exist in physical reality yet).

- Characters of stories (or equivalent components of other creative forms).

Spirits can be muses. The more you use them for inspiration, the more they see you as a partner, and the more inspiration they will provide you. You can also journey to a library or school, create a spiritual reality studio, or journey to interact with, or prototype, creations.

Creative Dreams

There is a long history of dream-based creativity in the arts and sciences, including:

1. Artists such as William Blake and Salvador Dali.

2. Authors such as Edgar Allen Poe, Dante, and Stephen King.

3. Film makers such as David Lynch, Federico Fellini, and Luis Bunuel.

4. Musical compositions like the "Devil's Trill Sonata" by Tartini and Handel's Messiah.

5. Mathematical proofs (Ramanujan was shown proofs in dreams by a Hindu Goddess).

6. Scientific theories such as Bohr's structure of the atom (he dreamed of electrons orbiting a nucleus, Kekule's molecular structure of benzene (he dreamed of a snake chasing its tail), Mendeleyev's periodic table, and Einstein's Theory of Relativity.

We can facilitate creativity in dreams by setting appropriate intentions. Dream creativity is easier for those who are capable of lucid dreaming, but if you are not proficient at lucid dreaming, shamanic journeying is a good way of starting to work with creativity.

Healing with Creations

We can also use creations in healing. The act of creating, or viewing, artwork can put you or an observer into an altered state of consciousness, facilitating spirit connection and healing. There are many examples across cultures of the use of creativity in healing:

- Navajo sand paintings are used in healing when a person sits on them, with the painting being the doorway through which spiritual power comes into the person.

- The Etruscan practice of creating sculptures of healthy organs for people with diseased organs to keep and visualize, assisting their healing.

- Creating prayer scrolls to be hung in homes of sick people to help manifest prayers.

- The South American practice of using songs (icaros) to heal or weaving song in fabrics to be used in clothing or hangings that sing healing energy into a person or space.

- The Mexican practice of creating healing art from beads and yarn containing symbols of spirits helpers as medicine for protection and power, or to manifest prayers.

You can journey to get healing symbols, songs, or words from spirit and paint these on a person or object or embed them in artwork. By creating a shamanic artwork or experiencing it as viewer, a person can receive healing. There is a potential issue here though. Such artwork may affect people that we do not have permission to work with. You might take the view that permission is not needed, or that people affected are those who are supposed to be. Does this overcome the issue or is this another example of well-intentioned sorcery?

Working with Creativity
There are several ways we can work with creativity, using guided meditation, creative visualization, dream work, or journey. You can remove creative blocks, including believing you do not have creative ability, being unwilling to embrace the unknown, being too attached to outcomes, allowing your conscious mind to filter out creative inspiration, being too focused on structure, and being influenced by norms and ideas of conformity.

Creative workshops are usually concerned with the mechanics of writing, painting, or musical composition. Shamanic creativity is different. You recognize a creation is alive and has a spirit that you can work with, or that you can get other input about a creation to help manifest it.

Stories are used here as an example, for other creative modes just change the intention accordingly. For instance, if you want to work with artwork journey to the Master Artist.

Different types of journey, or dream, intention can be used. You can journey to archetypal spirits, such as a Master Storyteller, or specific spirits such as the spirit of a dead author. You can also work with archetypal or individual spirits of a type of creation or a specific creation. You may even interact with stories of characters in a story to get their input on how they should be represented and their story arc.

You can seek ideas for a project or, if you already have a story idea, you can seek guidance or further input. Use books in a library to look up information. In journey a book may present information in picture or video form, and you can use its pages as a portal.

We can also get more general or specific advice about a particular mode of creativity and can undertake a variety of journeys to work with spirits or created works. You can set up a studio, in physical and/or spiritual reality. You can also establish a creativity altar, a place where you can get inspiration directly from spirit.

If you are stuck you can use other resources in a library to help you, like a catalogue or online search engine, or approach a librarian spirit and ask for help. You could also visit another institution like a writing school by modifying the intention.

As time is not linear it is possible to journey to the future to see a completed artwork that you will create for inspiration or to get ideas. If you regard this as cheating, consider that you are responsible for originally creating the work that you are journeying to observe!

Key Ritual: Journey to Meet the Master Storyteller

The intention is to journey to the Master Storyteller (or equivalent), an archetypal figure who represents all storytellers to ask for advice.

Aura

I was moving through a forest but paying attention to details like every leaf, everything moving, every frog, etc.

I said I want to see the master storyteller and I got the message that everything has a story, and everything is the storyteller if you want to listen. I felt it is one story with many versions.

It is a very strange feeling that everything is connecting into one single story and I was in there somehow floating in that story. Basically, it was like just be the story, it is there, listen and feel. Just listen to everybody and feel and the story is there.

It was feeling not really seeing except the very detailed forest and mountains popping in were detailed and telling me something. I remembered when I wrote something it felt good in my mind but not when I read it out. I was told, "Write for yourself, it is not authentic if you do not do that."

How to Do the Key Ritual

Here you journey to the archetypal figure of the Master Storyteller. Intend to go to meet them or ask one of your helping spirits to take you to them. As stated, if you are interested in another creative form, then substitute the archetypal spirit that you intend to visit. For example, if you want to work with art then intent to go to the Master Artist. The spirit will typically give you some general advice and you may get other visual input as in the example.

Other Rituals

Other rituals that you can perform include: journey to find out your creative mode, journey to meet a storyteller, journey to a spiritual reality studio, journey to a spiritual reality library or school, and journey to hunt or be hunted by a story.

You could also journey to meet a spirit muse, journey to find out how to improve your creative flow, journey to sources of inspiration, journey to find and remove creative blocks, journey to artistic ancestors to learn about creativity from them, journey to a story guardian, journey to the spirit of a character in a story, or journey to see or experience a completed creation or read a review about it.

Journey to Find out Your Creative Mode

The intention is to journey to find out what your creative mode is, what form your artistic expression takes. You may also receive specific advice about how to use this mode.

Ann

I went to the upper world. I was shown an intricate weaving. I was told it is time to refresh my creativity, not necessarily for money, and I know that I am to work with fabric. I was shown rolls of silks and satins in all sorts of colors. I was told not to worry about the outcome, just do it for fun and for generating creative juices.

Then I saw beautiful fabric, all different colors, reds and golds and things, like Aladdin's cave, awesome. I was shown some children's jackets that were simple but fabulous. Choose color and the feel of anything that you like to get your creative juices flowing.

Journey to Meet a Storyteller

The intention is to journey to meet a storyteller (or equivalent) to get advice on how they created stories and to see what advice they have for us. This could for instance be the spirit of a dead author.

Ryan

I went to Hemingway and asked him what I could learn. He said to use simple language, no more than three points or ideas per sentence. Give people detail but keep it central to the story. Introduce characters and involve them in the story. He said writing is a skill and you need to practice by writing in a journal. When you get bored or run out of material, go and seek out new adventures and material or characters.

Journey to a Spiritual Reality Studio

The intention is to journey to visit or create a spiritual reality studio you can use to create things. You can fit this out as you would a physical reality studio but are not constrained in the same ways and can use creative license to construct a studio. Such a studio could serve as a blueprint for a physical reality studio or a place to try out things before manifesting them.

Ludivine

I was in a tree house in the forest and it was the most beautiful place, so serene. I could see myself writing here for months and just watching the birds. I could even picture the spirit animals; it was just perfect.

During the journey I saw children playing on the beach and they were dressed up like in the early twentieth century. I thought that might be the subject of the book. A beautiful Amazonian bird with a big tail was there. It was great to be there.

I was asking to be shown the subject of the book, what is it about. I saw some water and I was in very blue water. At the end I saw a small boat on the ocean. I have always dreamed of going around the world on a boat.

Journey to a Spiritual Reality Library or School

The intention is to journey to visit a spiritual reality library or school to obtain information or conduct research, etc. Here we use books or other research materials to undertake research relevant to a forthcoming creativity exercise and obtain guidance or inspiration.

We can visit this library at any time in a journey or dream to undertake research. You can seek ideas for a creation project, or if you already have a project or story idea in mind you can seek guidance or further input. Use the books in the library to look up information.

A book can have special qualities. It may present information in picture or video form, and you may be able to step into one of its pages and use it as a portal. If you are stuck you can use other resources in the library to help you, like a catalogue or online search engine, or approach a librarian spirit and ask for their help.

There may be other people in the library. Can they help you?

Ann

I went to the upper world; an enormous being appeared in front of me. He was holding a religious wall hanging which was really beautiful.

I asked who he was, and he said, "I am the guardian of spiritual textile works." He looks after textiles in churches and monasteries and things. He said, "You need to research the works, you can go on to the computer, you do not have to go to places."

I said, "What period of history?"

He said, "Do not worry about the date, the date isn't important, the country is." He told me to look into Tibetan artefacts, and not to hang about, just get on the computer. He said, "What you are looking for is something that attracts you, color combinations and symbols; cut out a frame and use it to identify a section to replicate." He said the color combination is very important as I am sharing the spiritual works in sections.

I have got to choose it in the right way, trusting my intuition. He said to go and choose fabrics that appeal to me and make something which can go onto a cushion or the back of a jacket, etc. I am to be very specific about what I choose. The symbols and colors looked fantastic. It is the energy of the combination that is being put together spiritually. I am going to be sharing what is going to eventually die. I was told to do it for fun and not worry too much about it.

Journey to Hunt or Be Hunted by a Story

The intention is to journey to look for a story (or equivalent). The story may hunt you instead.

Aura

It was strange. It felt like some dark story of destruction. Everything was dark, volcanoes were exploding everywhere and there was like a wind howling like the sound wind makes through tunnels. It was strange in that world. I was moving through things. It felt tribal. There was a creation, a new thing coming up, so the destruction was creating something else. There were people drumming, it was very primal. The story was about the relationship between creation and destruction. You cannot create without destroying or destroy without creating. Things are supposed to be simple; I am the one complicating them.

Pro Tips

The following tips are provided:

1. **Choose to create.** If you do not create you allow your life to be created by others.

2. **Focus.** When you are engaged in creation focus on the creative process itself rather than on the intended creation, allowing creation without attachment to outcome.

3. **Extend creativity.** You should extend the creative process and intentions into other aspects of your daily life, such as your vocation and relationships.

4. **Symbols.** In any creative process you can use your symbolic language experienced in journeys and dreams to convey complex multi-dimensional information and wisdom. You may also be given new healing symbols by spirit.

5. **Childlike behavior.** One key to creativity is to work from a child's perspective of the world, which is viewed as full of wonder and a place for joy and playfulness.

DEATH

Death is often feared and viewed negatively, but shamans recognise that death is an ally who helps your transformation to a new life. In shamanic cultures there is no concept of eternal reward or punishment depending on behavior. Common ideas about death are shown in near-death experiences (NDEs) and reincarnation beliefs.

Our physical body may return to the earth, a part of us may remain in nature, but our essence returns to spiritual reality, from where we may be reborn. Many initiatory rites were designed to take initiates through a symbolic death to let them become familiar with death and be reborn as a new person.

Death Traditions and Mythology

Many cultures have maps of the journey taken after death, and texts or oral traditions that contain information and rituals for how to live and how to work with the dying and the dead. Main texts are the *Tibetan Book of the Dead* and the Egyptian *Book of the Dead*. Such traditions provide advice about how to live and die well, and rituals that can be used before death to ease fear and anxiety, and after death to guide the dead. Maps or descriptions of the journey into the afterlife were often provided as pictures, or texts, that were read to the dead.

Motifs seen in mythology and folklore include a difficult crossing that the dead take, such as spirit boats used to transport the spirits of the dead, a journey over a narrow bridge or between objects like clashing stones (the symplegades in Greek mythology). Such a crossing should be done swiftly and without fear. There are also myths of a descent to the underworld, typically taken to rescue a person who has been kidnapped by an underworld spirit.

What Happens at Death

People withdraw in the period before death and focus on what they want to do before they die. They have less energy. This may be due to illness, eating and drinking less, and irregular breathing that causes lower oxygen and higher carbon monoxide blood levels. This causes them to sleep more and movement, speech and thinking to slow.

As death gets closer a person begins to lose their senses as their body starts to shut down. They drift in and out of consciousness but retain a sense of hearing, which is why you are encouraged to talk to the dying even if they seem asleep. After death, our brain shuts down and we move from physical reality into spiritual reality. A person may retain awareness after death, helping them to move through the transition, or become more conscious later.

The spirit of the person may go to their destination in the upper or lower world of their own accord or may be helped by a psychopomp. They may meet the spirits of relatives and friends and participate in a life review. Their next stage is discussed and agreed with helping spirits.

The Near-Death Experience (NDE)

NDE experiences have consistent common elements which are similar to shamanic journeys:

- Hearing sounds like buzzing, ringing, music, wind or roaring.
- Sensing they are outside their body, able to see and hear events.
- Being outside normal time and space.
- Knowing they are no longer alive and may have died.
- Feeling peace and bliss.
- Moving through a tunnel to an area of intense golden or white light.
- Hearing celestial music.
- Being met by or seeing spirits.
- Taking part in a life review, with no judgement or punishment.
- Being told they have an unfulfilled destiny.
- Being reluctant to return to physical reality.
- Experiencing a barrier that they cannot pass or being advised they must return.
- The experience being powerful and not possible to easily describe.

A person who has an NDE often returns with different attitudes about life and death, including a desire to live fully and altruistically, increased compassion and love for others, and a reduced fear of death. People may also have increased psychic abilities. People who experience NDEs often make life changes, with many feeling a desire to work in helping or service professions.

Those who experience an NDE may struggle to with the experience. They can lose interest in physical reality and want to return to the light where they experienced peace, ecstatic bliss, and acceptance. They may have out of body experiences, visions, or lucid dreams, where they meet helping spirits who can provide support, advice and healing.

Things that you can do if you are struggling after an NDE experience include discussing your experience with others who have experienced the same thing or support professionals who are familiar the NDEs, reading books about the experiences of others, taking part in shamanic training or seeking help from shamanic practitioners, and asking helping spirits to assist you.

Working with Death

Our ancestors lived more authentically and observed rituals that enabled people to resolve issues before death and complete their journey to the after-life (meaning fewer spirits became stuck as ghosts). Now people do not live or die well, causing an increasing backlog of ghosts.

You can help people live authentically, express their life purpose, review and resolve aspects of their life, and view death as an ally. You can familiarise a dying person with what happens after death easing their transition and perform rituals to assist this or to comfort the bereaved. Examples of rituals for the dying include teaching them to journey to go to the light and experience what is waiting for them, or to guide them through a visualization of this process.

Such rituals are used to assist those dying or to help the bereaved. Here rituals are concerned with your understanding death, and symbolic death and rebirth.

Shamanic death and rebirth initiations typically involve a candidate shaman being left in wilderness and exposed to danger. Sometimes the candidate is buried in the earth. What needs to die in the person is let go of and changes occur that allow new things to come in, and the person to be reborn as a shaman. This may involve obtaining new spirits, typically from nature, who live in a shaman's body and become personal allies and power sources. After a shaman's death these spirits become disembodied and return to nature.

For yourself you might ask for *symbolic* death and rebirth. This is an initiatory ritual.

Key Ritual: Journey to Ask for Death and Rebirth

The intention is to ask your helping spirits for symbolic death and rebirth.

Lucie

I felt heavy compression on my chest, and they were opening it and taking something, while in the spirit world I was experiencing something fantastic. It was very different. I sat in an ice cave and I saw everything around me melting down.

Maybe it is a sign that I should so the same, so I thought, "Okay, let's melt down." So, I am pure lava and liquid at the same time, and I go through a long tunnel. I don't know where I am going. I lose a lot along the way until I am the tiniest ball, the essence of me being a small ball, a ball of light. When I understand that I reached the moment of being just me, I grow back into something that is like water, but different.

I go back into a tunnel that is going out, like a birth canal. All I can see is a third-person perspective of myself. I am like a water tiger. The spirit said I am reborn into something much stronger. I have always thought that I needed more water. They asked me to experience my new body, so I go into a dark jungle and everything I touch flourishes.

Then they said, "Now you understand that you are here to heal, everything you touch in the environment will heal by itself. Understand that. The more you get into this, you will not even need to touch things; they will just heal."

How to Do the Key Ritual

Here you will journey to have a symbolic death and rebirth experience. You are seeking transformation. You do not want to have an intention that is too specific, as you are limiting the potential outcome. You should have an open intention about what in you should be transformed and what it is transformed into. The intention stated above, to ask for symbolic death and rebirth, is such an open intention.

Be guided or ask to be taken to a suitable location. This could be a place in nature such as a cave or a forest, or one of the places that human souls go when a person dies. Be open to let go of old patterns and blocks. Let any negative emotions or behavior go, forgive others and be open to compassion and connection. Allow what needs to die within you to do so. Be open to transformation.

You may well meet spirits who will perform this initiation. This may involve experiences of dying symbolically. Do not be afraid of what is happening, but trust that experiences are in your best interests. Allow new capabilities to come in. As part of rebirth, you are healed. You are a new person. You have abilities and gifts that you did not possess before. You may receive insight into your authentic life purpose, the highest destiny that you can attain in this life.

After this journey you can journey to a power animal or other helping spirit to ask for explanation of or about guidance about events in the journey or things that you learned.

Other Rituals

Other rituals that you can perform include: journey to meet death, journey to see what happens after death, and journey to meet somebody you know who has died.

There may be used by a practitioner, or a dying person, to find out about and work with death. Other rituals may be used to assist the bereaved.

Journey to Meet Death

The intention is to journey to meet death. Ask a power animal or helping spirit take you.

David

It was not scary. It took time for me to meet death. It started with a tunnel with some light. He had no head. I asked him what I should know, and he told me that death is just a release and to help us to close a chapter, and it is necessary. When you are in the world it is because you are supposed to do something, and when everything you are supposed to do is done there is no need for you to remain in the world.

Journey to See What Happens After Death

The intention is to journey to be shown what happens when somebody dies. You may be shown events at or beyond death. Do not interfere in any way.

Sam

I saw a young girl come out of her body. She doesn't realize she is dead. She goes to see people she likes and after a while knows she is dead. Her angel appeared and held her. She goes with the angel to a big hall with golden light. There are many people and rooms here, with people teaching. She sat down, discussing things with others. She sits trying to remember. Finally, when she remembers many things her Angel took her to another hall. Many people queue up here to tell their story to somebody else.

Journey to Meet Somebody You Know Who Has Died

The intention is to meet somebody to obtain closure for one or both parties and to get a message from the spirit of the dead person. Sometimes the spirit of a dead person appears in a dream which may be an omen that they wish to be contacted. Try not to contact the very recently departed as the spirit needs time to arrive at their destination and adjust.

James

I met my father who died eighteen months ago. He looked younger and was joyful. I said I want to know where my grandmother was; he said she was fine but that is not for now. He had dogs with him. He said he didn't fully understand me when he was alive, but now he does. We went to a library and he got a book out to show me stuff.

Lucie

I saw my whole childhood in one second. I didn't see all of it, but I had the same feelings coming back. It was a really powerful feeling. I started crying because I was meeting my father. He didn't tell me that much that was new to me, things that he had told me before. He said he was in a good place and was watching me. He knows what I am doing and sees my daughter. He understands that I have my own family. He is very proud to see that my daughter and I are doing well.

Pro Tips

The following tips are provided:

1. **Rituals do not replace medical care.** Rituals are not meant to replace medical or hospice care. The physical needs of a dying person and pain management take priority.

2. **Release the dead.** The living must not try and keep hold of the dead and let them go to their destination. Holding on to them is one reason people get stuck as ghosts.

3. **No judgment.** Nowhere in death work should there be judgment of the deceased.

4. **There is no Hell.** Our notion of Hell is an invention used to control people through fear. Believing in Hell gives the concept power. Suicides do not go to Hell.

5. **Death is an ally.** We should see Death as an ally, not an enemy that we are afraid of. This allows you to live a life without fear, a life full of wonder and infinite possibility.

CONCLUSION

This book has focused on introductory work, with particular reference to rituals that a solitary practitioner can perform to explore shamanism. If you feel that you want to explore shamanism further, some next steps, reading and other resources are given below.

If you are seeking a shamanic practitioner or teacher, you can find details of recommended individuals on websites like those of the *Foundation for Shamanic Studies* and *Society for Shamanic Practitioners* which are provided in the other resources section.

Next Steps

Next steps you can take include:

1. Starting to work with your helping spirits to design your own journeys.

2. Reading more about specific topics that interest you (selected texts and other resources are recommended in the *Further Reading* section).

3. Find a shamanic teacher or drumming circle where you live.

4. Enrol in shamanic classes which you attend in person or join online.

5. Change your focus from working on your own development to working for others.

Further Reading

The following books are recommended as further reading:

Abrams, Jeremiah and Connie Zweig, eds. *Meeting the Shadow*. New York: Tarcher, 1991.

Berman, Phillip L. *The Journey Home*. New York: Pocket Books, 1996.

Cowan, Tom. *Shamanism as a Spiritual Practice for Daily Life*. Berkeley: Crossing Press, 1996.

Eliade, Mircea. *Shamanism, Archaic Techniques of Ecstasy*. Princeton University Press, 2004.

Farmer, Steven D. *Healing Ancestral Karma*. San Antonio: Hierophant Publishing, 2004.

Hall, Judy: *The Crystal Bible*. Iola, WI: Krause Publications, 2003.

Harner, Michael. *The Way of the Shaman*. San Francisco: Harper, 1990.

Ingerman, Sandra. *Soul Retrieval: Mending the Fragmented Self*. New York: HarperOne, 2006.

Moss, Robert. *Dreamgates*. Novato, CA: New World Library, 2010.

Narby, Jeremy and Francis Huxley. *Shamans through Time*. London: Thames & Hudson, 2001.

Rysdyk, Evelyn C. *Shamanic Tools*. San Francisco: Weiser, 2014.

Other Resources

The following other resources may be useful in your further exploration of shamanism:

Foundation for Shamanic Studies: http://www.shamanism.org/

Society for Shamanic Practitioners: http://www.shamansociety.org/

The Four Winds: https://thefourwinds.com/

Sacred Trust: http://www.sacredtrust.org/

Sacred Hoop Magazine: http://www.sacredhoop.org/

Why Shamanism Now?: http://whyshamanismnow.com/

A BLESSING

As noted previously, in a shamanic blessing a practitioner asks spirit to give spiritual power to another. I offer a blessing for you.

May spirit protect and empower you

May you be gifted knowledge and wisdom

May your pain and illness be soothed and healed

May service you give benefit others

May you fulfill your destined life purpose

And when this your current life is complete

May you return to your home in the stars

To Write to the Author

If you wish to contact the author or would like more information about this book, please write to the author in care of Llewellyn Worldwide Ltd. and we will forward your request. Both the author and publisher appreciate hearing from you and learning of your enjoyment of this book and how it has helped you. Llewellyn Worldwide Ltd. cannot guarantee that every letter written to the author can be answered, but all will be forwarded. Please write to:

Mark Nelson
℅ Llewellyn Worldwide
2143 Wooddale Drive
Woodbury, MN 55125-2989

Please enclose a self-addressed stamped envelope for reply,
or $1.00 to cover costs. If outside the U.S.A., enclose
an international postal reply coupon.

Many of Llewellyn's authors have websites with additional
information and resources. For more information,
please visit our website at http://www.llewellyn.com.